The
Changing
Tides

Kitchen Press
1 Windsor Place
Dundee DD2 1BG

www.kitchenpress.co.uk

First published by Kitchen Press in 2024

Text © Roberta Hall-McCarron 2024

Roberta Hall-McCarron has asserted her right to be identified as the author of this work in accordance with the Copyright, Designs and Patents Act 1988.

Photography © Rebecca Dickson 2024

Designed by Clare Skeats

The publisher would like to thank Helen Glassford for the use of the following paintings:

> Front cover: *Sea Thrift, Isle of Harris*
> Spring: *Luskentyre, Isle of Harris*
> Summer: *Low Tide, Eolaigearraidh, Barra*
> Autumn: *Reef, Isle of Lewis*
> Winter: *Isle of Coll*

© Helen Glassford 2024
www.helenglassford.co.uk

All rights reserved. No part of this publication may be reproduced, stored in a retrieval system, or transmitted in any format or by any means, electronic, mechanical, photocopying or otherwise, without prior permission of the copyright owners.

ISBN 9781739174033

A CIP catalogue record for this book is available from the British Library.

Printed in Bosnia and Herzegovina

This book contains FSC certified paper and other controlled sources to ensure responsible forest management

Roberta
Hall-McCarron

The
Changing
Tides

A Cookbook

Photography by Rebecca Dickson

For my daughter Cara, the brightest light in every day.

Contents

6 Introduction
10 Skills

26 Spring
84 Summer
148 Autumn
208 Winter

276 Core recipes
284 Index
288 Acknowledgements

Introduction

The changing seasons are as reliable as the changing tides.
MITCHELL TURNER

When I started to think about the sort of cookbook I would write, I knew it would be for the 'at-home chef' – recipes for simple, tasty and memorable dishes, just how I like to cook at home and yet still true to who I am as a chef. I wanted to take the reader on a voyage through the seasons. Like the changing tides, the seasons ebb and flow, and the flavours they bring with them are so important to the way I cook.

Being aware of when produce is at its peak and eating it when it is bursting with flavour is a truly joyous experience. Fresh green vegetables in spring, sweet juicy berries in summer, earthy mushrooms in autumn and endlessly warming root vegetables in winter. If I was asked to pick a favourite, I would struggle – the start of each season brings me so much excitement for the produce coming into my kitchen. Preparing ingredients that are only around for a few weeks is always a really special moment. The first grouse of the year is something I always look forward to. The short window for greengages. Elderflower starting to come out in Pilrig Park. This book aims to celebrate those moments. The produce in Scotland is exceptional – meat, game, shellfish, seafood, asparagus from Fife, strawberries from Perthshire, oysters from the west coast, the list goes on and on. It's a real pleasure to cook with and it inspires me every day to create dishes that taste fresh and delicious.

I often get asked the same question: what's your favourite thing to do when you're not working? It's quite simple – eat. I love getting together with friends and family, out in a restaurant or, even better, at home. For me, food is so much more than a necessity. It is the joy that it sparks when people get together over a meal – conversations are started, memories are made, a familiar flavour might take you back to another time.

In this book I've included recipes for all the ways I like to eat, from small snacky bites to brunches, big meaty feasts to sumptuous puddings. Some are simple, some a little more challenging, but they're always about celebrating the produce and having fun – my perfect recipe is one I have a good time making and an even better time eating. I enjoy taking classic flavour combinations and giving them their own little spin. Over the years, some of my best nights have been the dinner parties at home. More often than not the host gets stuck in the kitchen for most of the evening and misses out on all the fun but it doesn't have to be like this! At the end of each chapter, I've included a fun seasonal dinner party menu designed so it's easy to make a showstopper meal that everyone can relax and enjoy, including the chef. But you don't, of course, have to stick to my suggestions – feel free to use this book however you like, take an element from one dish and enjoy it with a sauce or side from another. There are no rules.

Scotland is a magical place. I've always been proud to say I'm Scottish. It's a beautiful country, steeped in history and breathtaking landscapes. Growing up, I spent a lot of holidays up north in the Highlands and on the west coast. My dad was a keen sailor and kept a boat at a small village called Ardfern, and many of our sailing trips involved some incredible food experiences. We would often sail to a random island just because my dad knew of a wee pub or restaurant there that was worth a visit: we'd anchor the boat, throw the dinghy in the water, go ashore and sample the wares. From pints of prawns and garlicky langoustines to deep-fried scallops off the pier at Tobermory, we ate well growing up. Our Scottish aperitivo would consist of sitting in the cockpit with friends from neighbouring boats, drinking and snacking on crudities and dips, which

would then lead to barbecues and water sports – the joy of bringing people together through eating and drinking.

When we weren't on sailing holidays, my sister and I would go with Dad to work every Saturday. He worked in the family business, Hall's of Broxburn, that made everything from sausages to bacon and pork pies. I was surrounded by food so it was perhaps inevitable that I would do something with food myself, but it was only when I was 16 that I came to this conclusion. At school, I had to do a week's work experience and it was my parents who suggested trying hospitality, so I spent a week in the kitchen at The Tower restaurant in the National Museum of Scotland. I was instantly hooked! I loved everything about it – the smells, the food, the passion, the creativity and just the crazy buzz of a busy kitchen. It was electric. Whilst I finished school, I continued working at The Tower part-time, then went to catering college in Glasgow, followed by a stint at the Balmoral. I had itchy feet though, and applied for a job at The Burj Al Arab in Dubai, 'the world's only 7-star hotel', and six short weeks later found myself moving to the U.A.E. I was only 22, and I needed a pep talk from my aunt to get me through a mini meltdown at Heathrow, but off I went. It certainly took some getting used to – the kitchen was very multicultural and it was a serious operation – and Dubai confirmed to me just how good the produce in Scotland is: I was amazed to see we served Scottish shellfish in the restaurant.

After a year and a half I started to get homesick, so I moved back to Edinburgh and started working at The Kitchin, which had only been open for about 9 months and had already won a Michelin star. Looking back, this was a pivotal moment in my career: it was infectious working in a restaurant where the chef owner was there for every service, unbelievably driven and passionate about Scottish produce and classical cooking. I was completely out of my depth and it was a struggle, but I was determined to succeed and learn as much as I could from Tom Kitchin and his team. After three and a half years I was ready for a change and was offered the position of sous chef at Castle Terrace, the new sister restaurant to The Kitchin. Dominic Jack was the chef patron there and had an unbelievable CV – he had worked at the highest level in France at both Taillevent and L'Arpege, and was a close friend of Tom Kitchin. He had been working at The Kitchin while he was looking for the right site for his restaurant, and I learned a great deal from him in the short time he was there so I knew this was the right move for me.

Castle Terrace will always hold a very special place in my heart. I was so proud to be part of its journey from the beginning – we achieved a lot in a short space of time, and a year after opening the restaurant it had its own Michelin star. I was gaining many of the skills that have helped through my career, not just in the kitchen but also learning how to manage a team. I met my husband, Shaun, who was the restaurant manager, and I gained my first head chef position. Many of the amazing people I met along the way – colleagues and guests – have shaped who I am and what I do. I was very lucky to have Dominic Jack and Tom Kitchin as mentors, and I spent a total of nine and a half years working for the group.

Shaun and I then spent a year and a half in Cambridge running a country pub with rooms before deciding to set up on our own, and we were soon back in Edinburgh looking for a site for our first restaurant. During this time, I briefly worked at Twelve Triangles bakery in Edinburgh. I didn't know much about baking but it was a fascinating diversion and it was the change of pace I really needed. I instantly became obsessed with bread-making and would bore Shaun to tears talking about hydration and showing him photos of cross sections of loaves. I learned so many wonderful things in my time there and have used so much of it in the restaurant that I would recommend any young chef spend some time in a bakery.

Two weeks after we got married in June 2018, we opened The Little Chartroom. Needless to say, it is all a bit of a blur. The name is a nod to those childhood sailing holidays. On our walls at home we had some of my dad's old shipping charts that my mum had mapped our sailing routes on to, so it made perfect sense for them to go up in the restaurant. I wanted guests eating in The Little Chartroom to feel like they were coming into my home and being greeted like old friends. I wanted it to feel special but also informal at the same time. The restaurant was born out of a passion for good, old-fashioned hospitality and delicious food that brings people together.

In 2020 we had to close the restaurant during the pandemic so we took the opportunity to open The Little Chartroom on The Prom, a food truck on Portobello beach offering tasty, simple and affordable food. The two chefs working there, Hamish and Moray, did such an incredible job out of an almost impossible kitchen setup that there were queues down the street so in 2021 we started looking for a second premises where The Little Chartroom on The Prom could become a proper restaurant. The Little Chartroom was even busier since I'd appeared on BBC Two's *The Great British Menu*, so it made sense for it to move to a bigger space, leaving the original site free for our second restaurant. The Little Chartroom 2.0 opened in September 2021, followed by Eleanore in December 2021. The name Eleanore also has a personal connection: she was the boat I grew up sailing on and there are illustrations of the boat in the restaurant. Hamish McNeill became the head chef – he is incredibly talented and had been working with us since early 2019 so it was an easy decision. By this time I was pregnant with my daughter, Cara, and was starting to prepare to take some time out, so Dominic Greechan took over as head chef at The Little Chartroom and the transition was seamless. Hamish and Dom are constant sources of inspiration to me, and this book wouldn't have been possible without them there to help me.

Taking time off after Cara was born was wonderful. It was incredible to get that time with her and adjust to a completely new way of life, and it gave me the opportunity to take a step back from the restaurant and allow the team to thrive and grow. I now look at the business in a different way: I can see the whole picture with no blinkers on and everything runs better for it. It's allowed me to travel and grow the business beyond Edinburgh – and it's allowed me the time to work on this book. I've always been a chef who adds a little bit of this and a little bit of that, so documenting it all properly has been a big challenge – a really good and positive one. I was asked repeatedly when I was writing the book which was my favourite dish and the answer was always the same, all of them. I've had the best time writing and creating *The Changing Tides*, and I hope you love it as much as I do.

Roberta x

Skills

I love being a chef. The learning is constant, we get to talk about, prepare and eat food all day, and even better we gain incredible skills, skills that I can't wait to teach my daughter. Having the knowledge to prepare fish and animals from start to finish is wonderful, and it gives you the tools to reduce waste and use as much of the produce as possible.

In this section I've covered some basic skills to help you prepare game and shellfish and fillet a fish, as well as a few other cooking basics like salting, smoking, poaching and toasting.

Shucking an oyster

Use a proper shucking knife for this job – a paring knife won't do; you'll probably just snap the tip off it.

Place the oyster curved-side down in a folded tea towel with the hinge facing away from you. Hold the oyster firmly and rest your hand on your work surface to keep it steady.

Stick the knife point in at the hinge, wiggling it and working it between the shells. Then twist the knife and prise the oyster open – sometimes you'll hear an audible 'pop'.

Now pull the knife across the inside of the top shell to release the oyster where it's attached. Lift off the top shell and place it to one side.

Turn the shell around in your hand and work the knife back and forth under the oyster, taking care not to pierce it, to release it from the bottom of the shell. Then use the blade of the knife to flip the oyster over to its smooth presentation side and brush away any fragments of shell.

Shucking a scallop

Use a flat knife or spoon with a thin, flat handle for this. Have a bowl handy to put your scallops in.

Hold the scallop with the hinge away from you. Insert the knife or the spoon handle into the side of the hinge and angle it upwards. Run the knife tip or spoon handle around the inside of the upper shell, keeping it as close to the shell as possible, until you feel the scallop muscle release. You can then pull the top shell off.

Use a spoon or a knife to scrape the bottom shell and release the skirt and roe and the other side of the muscle.

Gently scrape to release the scallop from the shell and slip it into your bowl.

Pick up the scallop and use your thumbs to work around the edges of it and tease it away from the skirt or 'frills' and black stomach.

Pull off any remaining muscle still attached to the scallop and remove the roe with your hands.

Place the scallop under under cold running water for 1 to 2 minutes to remove any waste or grit.

Cooking and breaking down a lobster

The most humane way to kill a lobster is with a knife. Using the tip of a sharp knife, carefully cut down through the head behind the lobster's eyes, angling the blade in the opposite direction from the body. You'll need to apply quite a bit of force; make sure you cut all the way through.

Snap off the lobster claws and place to one side.

Bring a large pot of salted water to a rapid simmer and carefully drop the lobster body in. Cook it for 3 minutes, then remove from the water and set aside to cool.

Lobsters have one claw bigger than the other. Bring the water back to a simmer and drop in the larger claw, then after 1 minute add the smaller one to the pot and cook for a further 2 minutes. Remove both claws from the water and set aside to cool.

Gently pull the lower pincer of a claw backwards to break it off – it should pull the inner cartilage out at the same time. Snap the lower pincer where the shell joins the claw, and pull off the shell so you can get to the meat inside.

Twist off the knuckle and set aside.

Using the heel of a knife, firmly tap the bottom part of the claw to crack the shell. Remove the shell and carefully pull the claw meat out. Check that the cartilage has been removed – if it's still there, carefully pull it out with your fingers.

Using a small pair of scissors, cut up each side of the knuckle and remove one side of the shell. Pull the knuckle meat out.

Twist the body and the tail in opposite directions to separate them. Turn the tail onto its side, press down with the flat of your hand to break the shell along the length of the tail, then pick it all off, keeping the tail meat in one piece.

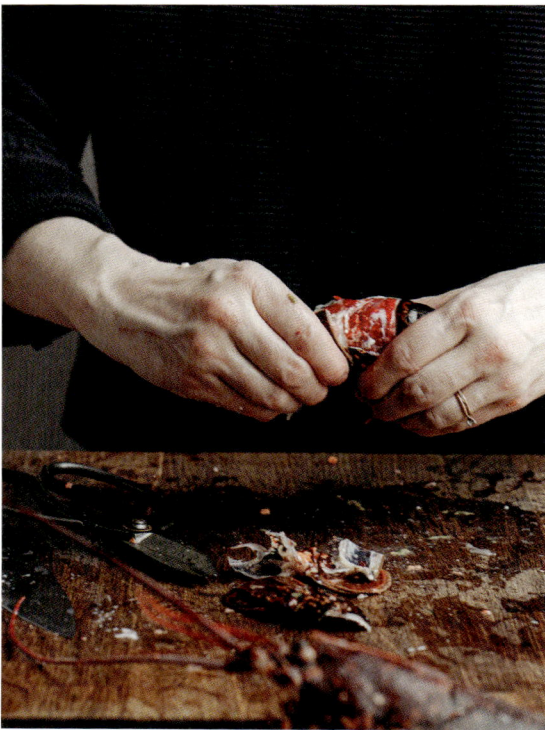

Filleting a mackerel

Use a long, sharp and flexible filleting knife for this. Have a bowl handy to put guts in, and kitchen towel will also be useful.

Place the fish with the stomach facing away from you on your chopping board. Hold the fish steady with one hand and with the other insert the knife tip into the underside of the fish between the two upper fins. Cut along the belly down to the hole.

Insert your fingers into the cavity and scoop out the innards. You will have to give them a yank to release them.

Feel along the spine for the blood line membrane. Pierce it and either scrape it out with your fingers or a knife or, alternatively, gently wash it out under running water. Use kitchen towel to wipe away any blood and dry the inside of the fish off.

Turn the fish over and cut off the pectoral fin (on the side of the body). This will make it easier to hold the fish steady when you cut into it.

Position the tip of your knife just behind the gills and make a confident cut down as far as the bone.

Turn the knife around, hold the fish steady and cut along the backbone to the tail.

Flip the fish over and cut through the skin next to the fin so the whole fillet is released.

Cut along the backbone again so the other fillet is released.

Cut along the bottom side of the fillet and then trim the top spine off.

Remove the translucent film that covers the skin by picking it loose at the corner and peeling it off. It will come away in one piece.

At the halfway point on the underside (the thinner side) of the fillet, slide the knife under and cut away the row of bones, using them to guide the knife.

Work your way down the centre of the fillet feeling for pin bones and tweezer them out. Have a little bowl of water nearby to drop bones in and clean your tweezers and fingers as you go. Remember to bone the top of the fillet too. A tip for removing stubborn bones is to pull down on them with the tweezers to loosen them and then pull up.

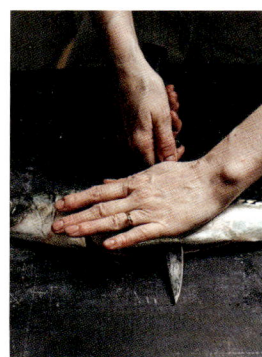

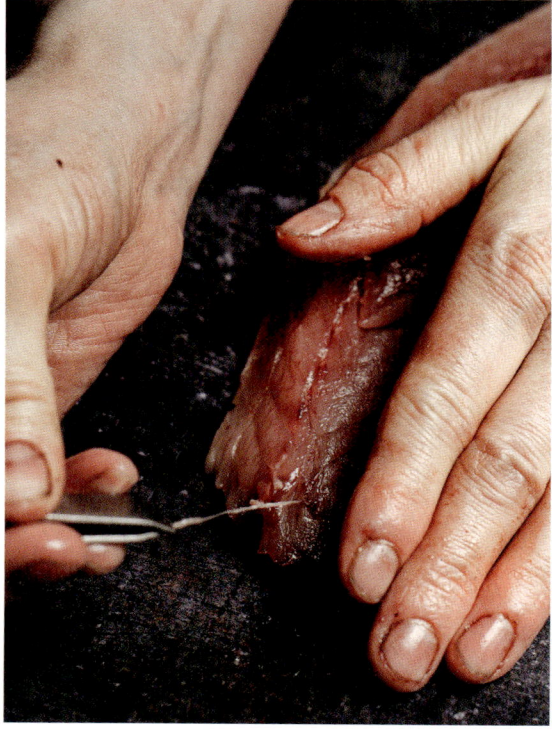

Prepping a game bird

Lie the bird on its back. Remove the head midway down the neck with a confident chop of a sharp cleaver.

Using your cleaver, tap the leg just above the foot so you break the bone but don't cut all the way through the leg. Repeat on the other leg. Now twist and snap each foot off and you should be able to pull the tendon from each leg.

To gut the bird, pinch the skin at the bottom of the belly and make an incision in the fold of skin.

Use two fingers to pull the cavity apart so you can access the guts. Insert two fingers and your thumb into the cavity, get hold of the guts and pull them out. Make sure you've got the heart and all traces of the intestines. The lungs sit on either side of the backbone on the inside of the ribcage and feel spongy. You should be able to hook them out with two fingers. You'll feel the bones at the back of the ribcage when you've successfully removed them.

Now remove the food sac. To access it, swivel the bird around and turn it over. Release the flap of skin from the bottom of the neck. Turn the bird back over and reach in and pull out the food sac (which may or may not be full) and the oesophagus.

Remove the wishbone. Peel off any stray bits of membrane to expose it. Make a shallow incision along the edges of the wishbone, insert the knife into the point where it meets the neck, then twist the knife and snap the bone. Do the same on the other side. Run the knife up the back of the bone to the top and pull it back, then get hold of it at the base and twist it off. Pull the skin back over.

Remove the rest of the neck with the cleaver.

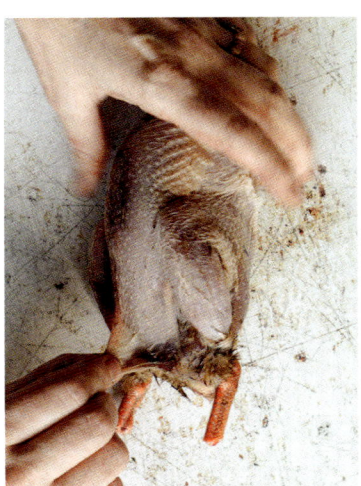

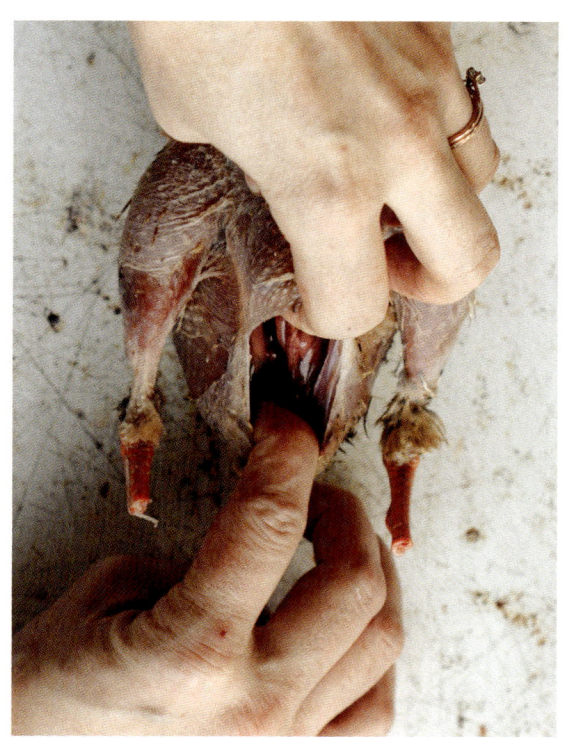

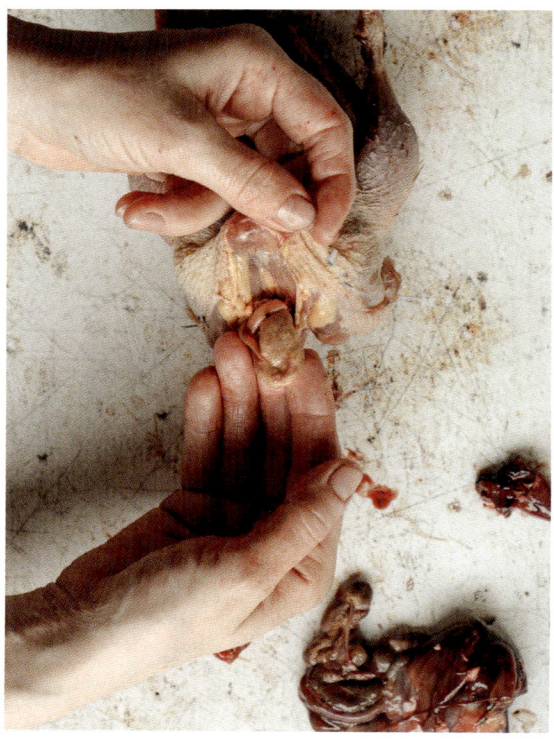

Tying a game bird

Position the bird on its back with legs facing away from you. Pull out string that is roughly four times the length of the bird but don't cut it from the ball.

Place the string under the bottom of the bird and cross it on top of the cavity but under the breast and pull it fairly tight. Hook the string behind each leg. Then turn the bird 90 degrees anti-clockwise and pull the string nearest you under the body and away. Do the same with the other end of the string, bring it round over the top and wind it round the body 3 times – you don't want it to be slack at all, but also it shouldn't be so tight that it cuts into the flesh. Cut the string and tie the loose ends in a double knot.

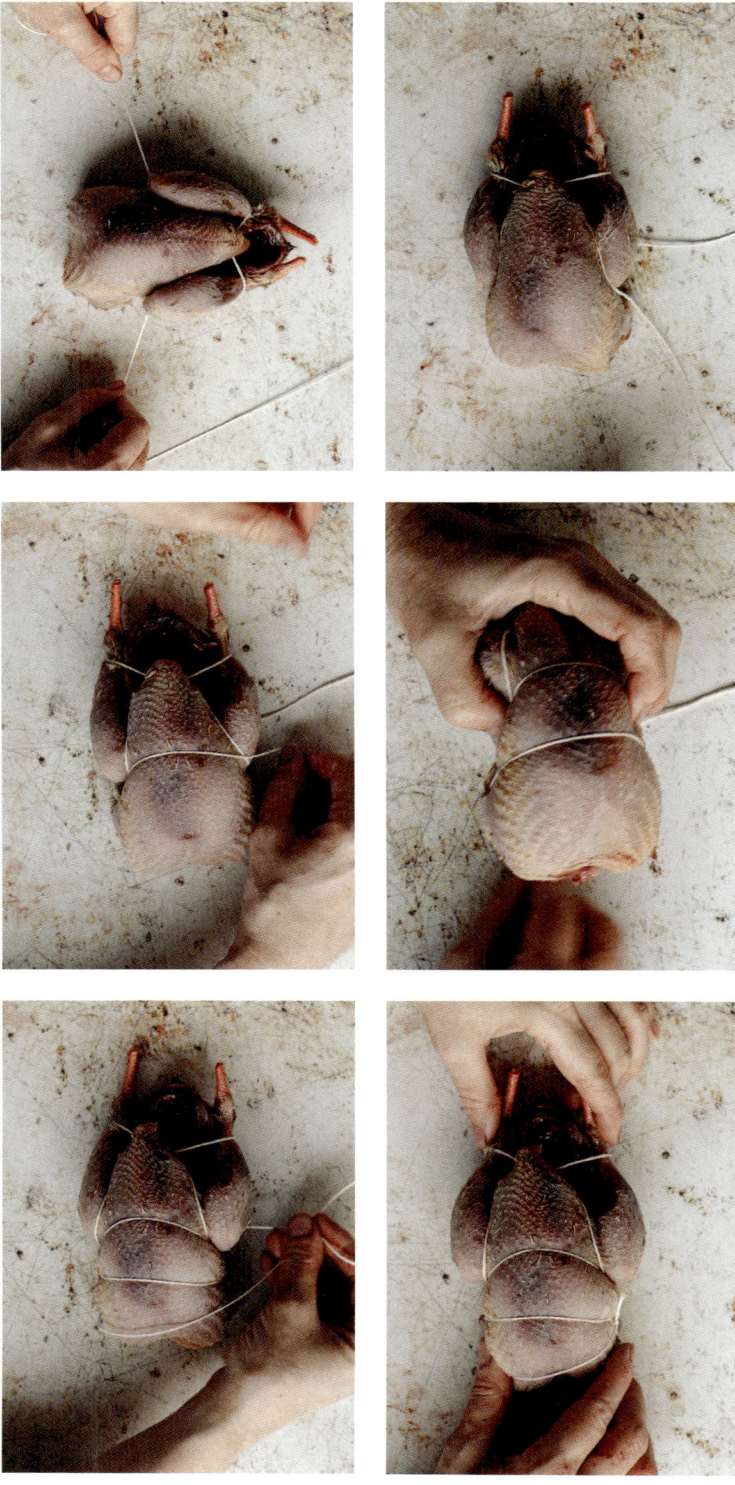

Smoking

I love the flavour smoking adds to any food, and you can incorporate different ingredients as well such as thyme, rosemary, tea, aromats – the list is endless. It's also very easy to do. You can smoke meat, fish, vegetables, butter, mayonnaise – anything you like really.

Hot smoking

This is how you get a smoky flavour into the food whilst cooking it at the same time, and it is particularly suitable for meat, fish and vegetables. It's the method used for the smoked duck and beetroot salad on page 218.

To hot smoke at home you need:

- a handful of wood chips
- 10g rice
- 10g thyme, rosemary or bay if you're smoking meat, or tarragon or dill if you're smoking fish

Make a tin foil bed in the base of a pot that a colander can sit on top of. Sprinkle the wood chips and rice over the tin foil, then lay the sprigs of thyme on top. Season whatever produce you are smoking, then lay them on a piece of greaseproof paper inside your colander. Put the colander over the pot and cover the whole thing with tin foil to keep the smoke in. Place the pot over a medium heat, and once the wood chips start to smoke leave for 10 minutes off the heat.

Cold smoking

When you just want a great smoky flavour, cold smoking is the best option. It's how I would smoke butter, mayonnaise, nuts, oils or the celeriac remoulade on page 199.

You'll need:

- a smoking tube
- 10g smoking chips
- a deep, heat-resistant tray big enough for a container and the smoking tube

Place whatever you're smoking in a heat-resistant bowl that fits inside your tray. Put the smoking chips in one end of the smoking tube and light them with a blow torch or over a gas flame. Lay the tube in the tray, near but not touching the bowl, and cover the whole thing with tin foil. Leave for 15 minutes.

Curing

You can preserve food by smoking, spicing, salting and brining but I really like to do a simple salt/sugar cure when I want to serve a 'raw' cold dish. I use a 50:50 ratio of salt and sugar and scatter it thickly all over the piece of fish or meat so it's completely covered.

The curing time will depend on the thickness of whatever it is you are curing. Some examples are:

    3cm thick sea bass fillet: 10 to 12 hours
    4cm thick trout fillet: 12 to 15 hours
    6cm thick halibut fillet: 12 to 24 hours

    3cm thick duck breast: 2 days
    4cm thick piece of venison: 2 to 3 days
    5cm thick beef fillet: 3 to 4 days

The cured produce will have a firmer texture than when it was raw.

Poaching an egg

Achieving the perfect teardrop-shaped poached egg with a soft runny yolk inside is easy; you just need plenty of water and vinegar.

Fill a deep pot with about 3 litres of water and add 240ml malt vinegar. (You want a ratio of 70ml of vinegar to every litre of water.) Bring to a rapid boil.

Crack your eggs into individual cups. Gently slip the eggs into the water one by one. Turn the heat down so the water isn't boiling but watch that it's not too low as the eggs might stick to the bottom of the pot. After 2½ minutes, carefully lift out your eggs and check them – you want them to feel soft but not so soft that they might break. If you don't think they're quite ready, get them back in and give them another 30 seconds. Fish the eggs out with a slotted spoon and drain on a piece of kitchen towel, then give them a wee trim with a pair of scissors and season with salt and a little bit of pepper.

Toasting nuts and seeds

I generally toast nuts and seeds in the oven as you get a nice even finish.

Preheat your oven to 170°c fan.

Spread the nuts on a baking tray and bake until golden brown (10 to 15 minutes), moving the nuts around halfway through.

Salting and brining

Salting or brining fish and meat really improves the produce by seasoning it throughout and locking in moisture that is often lost during cooking. It makes meat more tender and stops albumin (the white stuff that seeps out during cooking) forming in fish. It isn't a necessity – any recipe in the book can be done without the salting and brining process – but you will get a better result. It's up to you to decide whether you want to salt or brine: salting can help get a crispier skin if that's the result you're after, and brining increases the overall moisture content by approximately 20%. You can achieve moisture and crispy skin by brining first and then allowing the produce to air dry in the fridge.

Fish doesn't take long but meat requires at least 12 hours salting or brining time, so take this into consideration when planning recipes.

Salting fish

For 4 to 6cm thick fillets of fish like halibut or cod, you want to generously sprinkle fine salt on both sides and leave for 12 minutes. Leave thinner fillets of fish (sole, plaice, etc.) for 4 minutes. Wash the salt off in cold water and make sure it is all removed, then pat the fish dry with kitchen towel.

Salting meat and poultry

Use plenty of rock or sea salt and scatter it all over the joint or bird. Put it in the fridge overnight or for 12 hours, then wash the salt off with cold water and pat the meat dry with kitchen towel.

Brining

I usually use a 5% brine (50g of fine salt for every litre of water). You need enough to fully cover the fish or meat and a container big enough to put it in. For 3 litres of brine, heat up 200ml water in a small pot and add 150g fine salt. Stir until the salt has fully dissolved, then pour it into your container. Add the remaining 2.8 litres of water and stir to mix, then submerge whatever you are brining. Fish only needs to brine for 4 to 12 minutes depending on how thick it is. If you're brining meat, put it in the fridge and leave it overnight or for 12 hours. Pat dry with some kitchen towel – there's no need to rinse it – then put into the fridge for a couple of hours to dry.

Spring

My favourite times of year are at the start of each season, and spring is the one I yearn for the most as the days begin to get longer and lighter. Fresh, light, green early vegetables are such a beautiful contrast to the hearty root vegetables of winter.

Oysters with elderflower and cucumber

The sweet, acidic flavour from the elderflower vinegar is a lovely way to elevate an oyster.

We put a little damp salt on the plate to balance the oysters on.

SERVES 4

½ cucumber
30ml elderflower vinegar (page 276)
8 oysters, shucked
cold-pressed rapeseed oil
sea salt flakes

Peel the cucumber, then cut it in half lengthways and, using a spoon, scrape out the seeds.

Cut the cucumber flesh into small dice and put it in a bowl, then sprinkle with the elderflower vinegar.

Spoon a little of the cucumber on top of each oyster. Add a few drops of rapeseed oil and season with sea salt.

Whipped feta on toast with pickles

I've always got pickles in the fridge and here they work perfectly with the salty feta. Great as a snack or a light lunch.

SERVES 4

WHIPPED FETA
½ bulb of garlic, still in its skin
200g feta
100g Philadelphia cream cheese
1 tbsp double cream
zest of 1 lemon

PICKLES
10 radishes
6 baby golden beetroots
1 cucumber
1 recipe pickle liquor (page 280)
cracked black pepper
1 tbsp extra virgin olive oil

4 slices of sourdough bread

Preheat your oven to 170°c fan.

Wrap the garlic in tin foil and place on a tray in the oven. Roast for 40 minutes until the garlic is soft.

While the garlic is roasting, make the pickles. You need to keep all the veg separate so cut the radishes into quarters and put into a small bowl. Peel the beetroot, and cut each one into thin slices (about 2mm) and put into another bowl. Cut the cucumber in half across, then cut both pieces in half lengthways. Slice them into long ribbons about 5mm thick and put into a third bowl.

Pour enough of the cold pickle liquor over the cucumber and radish to cover them. In a pot, bring the rest of the liquor to a boil, then pour it over the beetroot and set aside to cool.

Unwrap the roasted garlic and leave it to cool before squeezing the soft garlic cloves out of their skins. Put the feta in a blender with the cream cheese, cream and lemon zest, and add the roasted garlic cloves. Blitz until smooth and scrape out into a bowl.

Toast or chargrill your sourdough slices, then spread generously with whipped feta. Top with a mix of pickles then sprinkle with a pinch of cracked black pepper and finish with a drizzle of extra virgin olive oil.

Smoked mackerel pâté with pickles and treacle soda bread

We started serving treacle soda bread in our second week of opening the restaurant, and it was an instant hit – to this day it's still the first thing you get when you sit down. It's very easy to make and the sweetness of the bread makes a perfect combination with a smoky mackerel pâté.

SERVES 4

SMOKED MACKEREL PÂTÉ
200g smoked mackerel
100g cream cheese
10g dill, picked
zest and juice of ½ lemon
40g crème fraîche

PICKLED CUCUMBER
¼ cucumber
100ml pickle liquor (page 280)

1 loaf of treacle soda bread (see below)

Remove any skin or bones from the smoked mackerel, then put it into a blender with the cream cheese. Blitz until you have a rough pâté – it doesn't need to be smooth. Transfer to a mixing bowl.

Finely chop the dill leaves and add to the mackerel pâté along with the lemon zest and juice. Fold through the crème fraîche.

Grate the cucumber through the big holes on a grater and put it in a bowl. Pour over enough pickle liquor to cover, set aside for 15 minutes and then drain.

Slice and toast the soda bread, then generously spread with mackerel pâté. Spoon over some pickled cucumber and serve.

Treacle soda bread

MAKES 1 SMALL LOAF

125g plain flour
125g wholemeal flour
75g large rolled oats, plus more for the top
1 tsp salt
1 tsp bicarbonate of soda
100g treacle
20g golden syrup
200ml buttermilk

Preheat your oven to 165°c fan. Line a baking tray with greaseproof paper.

Place the plain and wholemeal flours and the oats in a bowl with the salt and bicarb and mix well. In another bowl, whisk together the treacle, golden syrup and buttermilk, then pour the mix on to your dry ingredients and mix thoroughly to get a wet dough. (I find the easiest way is to use my hands.)

Transfer the dough to the lined baking tray and, using wet hands, shape into a loaf about 18 × 9cm. Sprinkle over a handful of oats.

Bake for 40 minutes, then transfer to a cooling rack and leave to cool before slicing.

Chickpea pancakes with peas

A traditional dish from the south of France called socca, *chickpea pancakes are the perfect vessel for all sorts of toppings and are delicious at any time of day. I've topped these with grated Grimbister, an Orkney cheese with a lemony tang that works really well with the peas, but if you can't find it Parmesan will be as good. Use 40g store-bought pickled onions if you don't want to make your own.*

SERVES 4

PEA PURÉE
1 tbsp sunflower oil
1 small onion, thinly sliced
1 tsp sea salt
100ml vegetable stock
100ml double cream
200g frozen petit pois
40g baby spinach

PICKLED ONIONS (*if you want to make your own*)
40g baby onions
200ml pickle liquor (page 280)

CHICKPEA PANCAKES
90g gram/chickpea flour
1 tbsp extra virgin olive oil
¾ tsp salt
sunflower oil

300g fresh peas in the pod (150g podded weight)
2 tbsp pickle liquor (page 280)
extra virgin olive oil or cold-pressed rapeseed oil
sea salt
100g Grimbister cheese, finely grated
zest of 1 lemon

Start with the pea purée. Put the oil in a pan over a medium heat, then add the onion and salt and sweat down until it is soft and translucent. Pour in the vegetable stock and cream and reduce by half, then add the petit pois and cook for one minute until just defrosted. Take the pan off the heat and add the spinach, then blitz until you have a thick purée. Press a piece of cling film on to the purée to stop a skin forming and leave to cool.

If you want to pickle your own onions, peel the baby onions and put them in a small pot. Cover with the pickle liquor and bring to a simmer, then cook until the onions have softened and the liquor has reduced by half. Leave to cool.

To make the chickpea pancakes, put the gram flour in a bowl with the olive oil, salt and 150ml water. Whisk to get a smooth batter, then pass it through a fine sieve into a jug. Put a 15cm frying pan over a medium heat and add enough oil to just cover the base. Once it's warm, pour a very thin layer of the batter into the pan and cook for 2 minutes on each side. Repeat until you've used up all the batter.

Pod the fresh peas and blanch for 10 seconds in boiling, salty water. Refresh in ice water and drain. Dress the peas with 2 tablespoons of pickle liquor, a splash of either olive oil or cold-pressed rapeseed oil and a pinch of sea salt.

Spread a layer of pea purée over each of the pancakes. Scatter over some dressed fresh peas, then cut the baby onions into quarters and place on top. Finish with the finely grated cheese and a little lemon zest.

Scotch pies

Scotch pies were a staple for me growing up, and these smaller bite-sized versions make the best snack! You can use pork belly with a good bit of fat through it if you have trouble getting hold of pork fat.

MAKES 20 PIES

HOT WATER PASTRY
520g plain flour
2 eggs
160g lard
1 tsp salt

FILLING
250g lamb mince
125g pork fat, minced
1½ tsp salt
½ tsp ground mace
½ tsp ground nutmeg
½ tsp white pepper

EGG WASH
2 egg yolks, beaten

8cm and 5cm pastry cutters

Start with the hot water pastry as it needs to rest for longer in the fridge than shortcrust. In a bowl, roughly mix the flour and eggs together. Put the lard and salt into a pot with 100ml water and bring to a boil. Pour this over the flour mixture and stir until you have a soft dough. Shape the dough into a fat disc, wrap in cling film and put in the fridge to chill for at least 3 hours.

The pie filling is simple: just mix the lamb mince with the pork fat, salt, mace, nutmeg and white pepper. Divide into 20 portions and roll each between your palms to shape them into balls.

Preheat your oven to 180°C fan and line a baking tray with greaseproof paper.

Roll out the dough to 4mm thick on a floured worktop. Cut out 20 circles of dough with the 8cm cutter and 20 with the 5cm cutter, then start to build your pies.

Brush one of the 8cm pieces of pastry with water, then place a ball of filling on top. Place a smaller circle on top of the filling and smooth it down with your hand. Bring the sides of the bottom piece up and join them to the top by pinching at five points. Make a hole in the top with a cocktail stick.

When you've done all the pies, brush them all over with egg wash, then put them on the greaseproof-lined tray. Bake for 15 to 20 minutes, until golden brown. Serve with a generous dollop of pickled walnut ketchup.

Pickled walnut ketchup

This makes more than you need but you can keep any leftovers in a jar in the fridge for two weeks.

MAKES 450ML

1 onion, thinly sliced
1 tsp sunflower oil
1 Bramley apple, peeled, cored and chopped
1 tbsp demerara sugar
390g jar pickled walnuts, drained and chopped
salt

Sweat down the onion in the oil until soft. Add the apple, then mix in the sugar and a pinch of salt. Finally, add the drained pickled walnuts and cook for about 10 minutes until the apples are very soft.

Blitz until smooth, then taste and adjust the seasoning if needed.

Herb gazpacho

Fresh, zingy and vibrant. Definitely one to be enjoyed on the first warm day in spring.

SERVES 4

1 cucumber, peeled and roughly chopped
1 green pepper, trimmed, deseeded and roughly chopped
20g mint, leaves picked
20g parsley, leaves picked
20g basil, leaves picked
½ garlic clove, thinly sliced
50g sourdough bread, torn into pieces
50g olive oil
1 tbsp sherry vinegar
1 tsp sea salt

TO FINISH

60g fresh peas in the pod (30g podded weight)
extra virgin olive oil
40ml crème fraîche
20g flaked almonds, toasted (page 23)
edible flowers
sea salt

Put the chopped cucumber and green pepper in a large mixing bowl. Tear the mint, parsley and basil leaves into pieces and add to the bowl, along with the garlic and sourdough. Pour over the olive oil and sherry vinegar, then add the sea salt and mix everything together thoroughly.

Leave everything to marinate for at least 2 hours (it can sit for up to 24 hours in the fridge). Transfer to a blender and blitz until smooth, then pass through a fine sieve into a bowl. Taste the gazpacho and adjust the seasoning accordingly, adding a little more vinegar if needed.

Pod the peas and blanch for 30 seconds in boiling, salted water. Refresh in ice water and drain, then dress in a splash of olive oil and a pinch of salt.

Pour the gazpacho into your serving bowls. Place a dollop of crème fraîche on top, then add a drizzle of olive oil and scatter over some peas, flaked almonds and edible flowers.

Wild garlic soup with smoked haddock and almonds

The flavour of wild garlic changes as the season progresses – mild and sweet at the start, punchy and strong by the end. I enjoy it best right in the middle.

SERVES 4

4 onions, thinly sliced
sunflower oil
1 tsp sea salt
200g potatoes, peeled and roughly chopped
1l vegetable stock
200g wild garlic
350ml double cream
120g smoked haddock
2 sprigs of thyme
2 fresh bay leaves
40g flaked almonds, toasted (page 23)

Gently sweat down the onions in a pot with a little oil and the salt until soft and transparent. Add the potatoes, give it a stir and then pour over the vegetable stock. Bring to a simmer and cook for 10 minutes, until the potatoes are tender.

Roughly chop the wild garlic and stir it into the soup. Cook for 1 minute, then add 150ml of the cream and take the pot off the heat. Carefully transfer the soup to a blender and blitz until it is smooth.

Place the smoked haddock in a pot with the remaining 200ml cream and the thyme and bay leaves. Bring to a simmer, then take off the heat and leave to cool for a few minutes. Discard the herbs, then strain the haddock through a sieve into a small bowl so you keep the smoky cream. You won't need all of the cream, but it's delicious mixed through some eggs so don't throw it away.

Divide the soup between your bowls and flake the smoked haddock on top. Drizzle over some smoky cream and finish with a scattering of toasted almonds.

Chicken and orzo broth

Growing up my mum would make cock-a-leekie soup a lot. My sister and I weren't big fans of leeks or prunes, so mum would make the base stock and finish ours with chicken and rice. I now eat everything and love making my own version of it, packed full of veggies. This recipe makes a big pot, but I keep it in the fridge and it's great for a couple of days.

SERVES 8

8 chicken legs, bone in
10g thyme
4 garlic cloves
2 bay leaves
1 tbsp sea salt
10g dried shiitake mushrooms
500g fresh peas in the pod (250g podded weight)
8 asparagus spears
120g orzo
150g chestnut mushrooms, halved and finely sliced
1 bunch spring onions, finely sliced
½ tsp cracked black pepper

Using a knife, separate the thighs from the drumsticks. You'll feel a dip where the two bones connect – just press your knife there and cut through.

Place the chicken thighs and drumsticks in a large pot and cover with 3 litres of water. Bring to a simmer and skim off any froth, then add the thyme, garlic, bay and salt. Simmer gently for 15 to 20 minutes.

Carefully fish out the chicken pieces and set them aside to cool. Pick the meat from the bones, removing any sinew or cartilage, then return the bones to the stockpot and simmer for 30 more minutes. Take off the heat and add the dried shiitakes, then leave to infuse for 15 minutes. Pass the stock through a fine sieve into a big pot.

When you're ready to eat, pick the chicken meat down into smaller pieces and pod the peas. Snap the bottom part of the asparagus off – it will naturally break where the woody part ends – and then cut the tips to 3cm and thinly slice the rest of the spear.

Warm the stock to a simmer. Add the orzo and cook for 8 minutes, then the sliced chestnut mushrooms and cook for another 3 minutes, then the asparagus and cook for 1 minute more. Stir through the peas, spring onions, black pepper and chicken and remove from the heat.

Ladle the broth into your serving bowls and finish with a spoon of salsa verde.

Salsa verde

MAKES ABOUT 100ML

20g parsley
20g tarragon
1 garlic clove
4 anchovy fillets
1 tbsp capers
1 tsp Dijon mustard
1 tsp white wine vinegar
1 tbsp extra virgin olive oil

Place all the ingredients in a blender and blitz. Have a taste and adjust the seasoning if required. You can also do it by hand: just finely chop the parsley, tarragon, garlic, anchovies and capers, then add the Dijon, white wine vinegar and oil.

Asparagus and roast chicken hollandaise

Asparagus is one of the most amazing vegetables – so versatile and so tasty! Dominic, our head chef at The Little Chartroom, put this dish on the menu and it's been a real hit: it is a classic with a twist. You'll need a couple of hours to get the chicken stock to the right place to make the hollandaise, but it's worth the wait.

SERVES 4

ROAST CHICKEN HOLLANDAISE
1.5l brown chicken stock (page 278)
2 eggs
25g double cream
1 tsp sherry vinegar
½ tsp salt
175g butter, melted

TO SERVE
1 bunch of asparagus

Pour the chicken stock into a large pot and bring to a boil over a medium-high heat. Keep it simmering away until it has reduced to 100ml: it can take a couple of hours to get the sauce-like consistency and very strong chicken flavour you're looking for.

Put 25g of the reduced chicken stock into a heatproof bowl with the eggs, cream, sherry vinegar and salt. Give everything a whisk to mix, then place over a bain-marie and whisk until the egg has aerated and thickened.

Gradually add the melted butter to the egg mix, whisking continuously. If the mix is getting too thick or looks like it might split, add in a splash of water. Taste and add more salt if necessary.

Snap off the bases of the asparagus spears and trim off the leaves with a small sharp knife. Either blanch them for 1 minute in boiling, salty water or drizzle them with a little oil, sprinkle with salt and chargrill for 2 minutes.

To serve, spoon a layer of hollandaise on to your plates, then top with asparagus.

Trout and spring vegetable galette

Galettes are delicious and simple and can have any topping you like. Danielle, a chef that used to work at the restaurant, made a great one for staff meal one day that consisted of cream cheese, potato and onion. I now make spinach, cream cheese and hot smoked trout versions for my young daughter at home. So tasty, and a lovely way to enjoy beautiful spring vegetables.

The pastry is very easy and delicious, but ready-made puff pastry is a great alternative if you're short on time.

SERVES 6

GALETTE PASTRY
180g plain flour
½ tsp salt
100g butter, diced small
80ml cold water
1 egg yolk, beaten

100g cream cheese
200g skinless trout fillet, cut into 2cm pieces
100g fresh peas in the pod (50g podded weight)
4 asparagus spears,
10 radishes, cut into quarters
1 small courgette, halved and thinly sliced
25g baby spinach
juice of ½ lemon
1 tsp cold-pressed rapeseed oil
sea salt

First, make the pastry. In a bowl or mixer, mix the flour and salt together, then add the butter and rub in (or blitz) until you have a breadcrumb consistency. Gradually add the water to form a dough, then mould it into a fat disc, wrap in cling film and place in the fridge to rest for an hour.

Preheat your oven to 175°C fan.

Once the pastry has rested, roll it out on a floured worktop to make a rough circular shape about 30cm in diameter and 5mm thick. Trim to a neat circle, then fold over the edges of the pastry to make a 3cm rim and brush the pastry with plenty of beaten egg yolk. Put on a baking tray, and bake for 20 to 25 minutes, until the pastry is cooked.

Spread cream cheese in a layer within the pastry rim and arrange the trout on top. Bake for another 4 minutes. Set aside while you prepare the vegetables.

Pod the peas and blanch in boiling, salty water for 20 seconds, then refresh them in cold water. Snap off the woody base from the asparagus spears, then blanch for 1 minute. Drain and leave to cool, then halve each spear vertically and cut each half into three. Blanch the quartered radishes for 30 seconds, then drain and leave to cool. Scatter a little sea salt over the sliced courgette and leave for 5 minutes.

Put the peas, asparagus, radishes and baby spinach in a bowl and dress with the lemon juice, rapeseed oil and a little sea salt. Arrange the vegetables on top of the galette, with slices of courgette tucked in here and there.

Scallops and sweetheart cabbage

Sweetheart cabbage stuffed with crab and orange is really delicious on its own or alongside any piece of fish, but it is extra special with a couple of sweet, perfectly cooked scallops.

SERVES 4

STUFFED CABBAGE
1 sweetheart cabbage
½ tsp fine salt
sunflower oil
50g panko
1½ tbsp nutritional yeast flakes
¼ tsp garlic powder
1 orange
100g white crabmeat
50g butter
5g dill, picked and finely chopped

SCALLOPS
8 large scallops, shucked and prepared (page 12)
sea salt
sunflower oil
50g butter

Cut the sweetheart cabbage into quarters lengthways, season with the fine salt and leave for 20 minutes.

Put a splash of oil into a frying pan and place over a medium-high heat. Put the cabbage in and sear until it has good colour on each side, then turn the heat down and cook for 4 minutes on each side, until it is cooked through. Put the cabbage on a plate and set aside.

In the same pan, add the panko, nutritional yeast flakes, garlic powder and a good pinch of sea salt with a splash of oil. Toast until golden brown, keeping the pan moving continuously. Set aside for now.

Using a small sharp knife remove the skin of the orange, then slice out the segments and discard the membranes. Cut the orange segments into very small (2 to 3mm) dice, keeping any juice that seeps out as you cut.

Check through your crabmeat for any shell. It's useful to have a small bowl with cold water when doing this as you can just drop any shell that you find into the water – it easily falls off your fingers. Gently melt the butter, then stir through the crab, orange and finely chopped dill.

Place a wedge of sweetheart cabbage on each plate and layer the crab mix between some of the leaves. Finish with a generous sprinkling of the panko mix.

Season the scallops with a little sea salt. In a hot pan with a little oil, cook the scallops for 2 minutes on each side. Turn the heat down and add in the butter: as it foams, baste the scallops for 1 minute and then remove from the pan. Place two scallops on each plate and serve.

Kedgeree

As I was working my way through the book writing the recipes, I joked with my husband that maybe we should have just brought out a book that had all the brunch dishes that we used to do, as there were so many favourites. Kedgeree was another regular on the menu – it's a very well-known dish and this is my version.

In the restaurant we smoke our own fish, which is really easy to do at home (see page 22). But un-dyed, smoked haddock from the fishmongers works perfectly too.

SERVES 4

1 onion, finely diced
sunflower oil
3 garlic cloves, grated
½ tbsp garam masala
½ tbsp turmeric
125g basmati rice
4 bay leaves
200ml double cream
200g smoked haddock fillets
zest of 1 lime
4 spring onions, thinly sliced
50g baby spinach,
10g coriander, leaves picked and roughly chopped
fine salt

TO SERVE

150g yoghurt
50g flaked almonds, toasted (page 23)
4 poached eggs (page 23)

In a pot, gently sweat the onion down in a little oil until soft and transparent. Add the grated garlic, garam masala, turmeric and a couple pinches of salt and continue to cook for 5 minutes.

Rinse the rice in a sieve under running water for a few minutes, until the water runs clear. Add it to the pot and stir so each grain is well coated in the spices.

Finally add two of the bay leaves and 200ml water, then cover with a lid and bring to a boil. Lower the heat and cook for 10 to 12 minutes until all the liquid has been absorbed. Remove the bay leaves but leave the lid on to keep the rice warm.

In a wide-bottomed pan, warm the cream with the remaining two bay leaves and a pinch of salt until it is steaming. Add in the haddock and gently poach for 2 to 3 minutes, then remove it with a fish slice and leave to cool a minute before flaking it.

Grate most of the lime zest into the rice, then stir through the sliced spring onions, baby spinach and coriander – the rice should be warm enough to wilt the spinach. Check the seasoning and adjust it if needed.

Spoon the rice on to your plates and scatter the flaked haddock on top. Add some dollops of yoghurt, the toasted almonds and your poached egg. Grate over a little more lime zest and enjoy!

Goat's cheese agnolotti with wild garlic sauce

When wild garlic is in season I use it as much as possible, and this is a very tasty way to showcase it.

SERVES 4

MUSHROOM STOCK
500g button mushrooms, sliced
1 tsp salt
a handful of dried porcini

AGNOLOTTI
220g goat's cheese
zest of 1 lemon
1 tsp fine salt
75ml double cream
5g chives, finely chopped
¼ tsp ground black pepper
1 recipe pasta dough (page 281), rested

WILD GARLIC SAUCE
50g wild garlic, stalks discarded
50g spinach, stalks discarded
25g flat-leaf parsley, leaves picked
40g crème fraîche

Begin with the mushroom stock. Put the mushrooms and the salt in a pot with 500ml water. Cover and bring to a simmer, then turn the heat down and very gently cook for 1 hour.

Turn off the heat and throw in the dried porcini, then leave to infuse for 10 minutes. Discard the porcini and pass the stock through a sieve into a bowl. Let the strained mushrooms get cool enough to handle, then finely chop half of them and discard the rest.

To make the pasta filling, mix the goat's cheese with the lemon zest, salt, double cream, chives and black pepper, then add the chopped mushrooms. Taste and add more salt if needed, then transfer to a piping bag.

Cut the pasta into two pieces, and wrap one of them back up in the cling film. Using a rolling pin, flatten the other piece so it's about 2cm thick, then feed it through the pasta machine on its widest setting. Fold in either end of the pasta sheet so you have a triple layer, then feed it through the machine again. Now, change the pasta machine to the next setting and roll the pasta through twice, without folding it. Roll it twice through each remaining setting, and you will have a long piece of pasta, thin enough that you can see your hand through it. Repeat with the other piece of pasta.

Put one of the sheets on your work surface, preferably wooden. Pipe a line of the filling about a third of the way up from the bottom of the pasta sheet. Using your finger, slightly wet the strip of pasta nearest you, then fold it over, firmly pressing to seal the filling in. With a pasta wheel, trim the excess pasta so you have a 1cm lip. Firmly pinch the stuffed pasta between your finger and thumb at 5cm intervals to make little pillows, then use the pasta wheel to cut between them, going from the folded side to the lip to get the distinctive agnolotti shape.

To make the sauce, blanch the prepared wild garlic, spinach and flat-leaf parsley in boiling, salted water for 30 seconds, then refresh in ice water. Drain, then squeeze out any excess moisture and put them into a blender with the reserved mushroom stock and the crème fraîche. Blitz until smooth, then taste and adjust the seasoning if needed. Put the wild garlic sauce into a pan over a low heat to warm.

Cook the agnolotti in simmering salted water for 4 minutes, until soft. Carefully remove from the water and put on to your serving plates, then pour over the warm wild garlic sauce.

Roast guinea fowl with peas and bacon

Peas and bacon – one of my favourite flavour combinations. Prepared and served this way, they're the perfect addition to elevate the humble roast. I often use Polish pork belly, boczec, *here instead of pancetta. It's easily available in the Polish section at the supermarket and it has a wonderful flavour.*

If you plan ahead and can make the space in your fridge, it's great to brine the guinea fowl and then leave it to air dry in the fridge for a couple of days. The meat will be beautifully seasoned and the skin gets extra crispy when it's cooked.

SERVES 4

ROAST GUINEA FOWL

150g salt
1.2kg guinea fowl
2 onions, roughly chopped
3 carrots, peeled and roughly chopped
2 celery sticks, roughly chopped
1 garlic bulb, cut in half across
10g thyme
6 bay leaves
1 tbsp sunflower oil
1 lemon, pricked all over with a skewer

PEAS AND BACON

1 small onion, thinly sliced
sunflower oil
100ml pork or ham stock
100ml double cream
300g frozen petit pois
40g baby spinach
600g fresh peas in the pod (300g podded weight)
100g pancetta (or Polish pork belly), diced
½ baby gem lettuce, thinly sliced

First, make your brine. Warm 200ml water in a pot and add the salt, stirring until it has dissolved. Add another 2.8 litres of water. Put the guinea fowl into a large container, and pour over the brine, making sure the bird is fully submerged. Leave it overnight in the fridge.

The next morning, drain the guinea fowl and pat it dry, then put it back in the fridge on a wire rack on a tray, for at least 6 hours and up to 2 days. Let it come up to room temperature for 35 to 40 minutes before cooking.

When you're ready to cook, preheat your oven to 200°c fan. Put the onions, carrot, celery and garlic bulb into a roasting tin, and mix in half of the thyme and three of the bay leaves. Rub the guinea fowl with the oil, then put the lemon and the remaining thyme and bay leaves into the cavity, and place the bird on top of the veg. Cook for 35 minutes, until the juices run clear, then set aside to rest for 30 minutes.

While the guinea fowl is resting, get on with the peas and bacon. Nice and gently, sweat down the onions in a little oil until they are soft and transparent. Pour in the stock and cream and turn up the heat to bring it to the boil. Reduce until the pan is almost dry, then mix in the frozen peas and spinach and cook until the peas have fully defrosted and the spinach is wilted. Take the pan straight off the heat and carefully transfer the mix to a blender. Blitz until smooth, then taste and adjust the seasoning.

Pod the fresh peas and blanch them in boiling, salty water until they rise to the surface. Sauté the pancetta with a little oil in a pan over a medium-high heat, until it is cooked and a little golden. Stir in the blanched peas and the sliced baby gem, and cook for 30 seconds, then add the pea purée and give it all a stir. Get it nice and hot and transfer to your serving dish, then put the guinea fowl on top to serve.

Baked John Dory with seaweed Jersey Royals

John Dory is one of my favourite fish; it has a really unique flavour. This is a very simple dish that allows the produce to shine.

SERVES 4

1 John Dory, weighing about 1kg
1 tbsp sunflower oil
sea salt

SEAWEED JERSEY ROYALS
500g Jersey Royals
1 tbsp fine salt
2 banana shallots, finely diced
sunflower oil
25g nori sheets
1 tbsp rice vinegar
½ tbsp honey
½ tbsp soy

Preheat your oven to 200°c fan.

Rub the John Dory all over with oil and season with sea salt. Place it on a greaseproof paper-lined tray and bake in the oven for 20 minutes.

Pop the Jersey Royals and tablespoon of salt in a pot and cover with cold water. Bring to a simmer and cook for 20 minutes until the potatoes are tender.

Sweat the shallots in a little oil for a few minutes, until nice and soft. Blitz the nori sheets and add to the shallots, then stir in the rice vinegar, honey and soy. Simmer for 5 minutes, until most of the liquid has evaporated.

Drain the potatoes, reserving the cooking water, and if they're big cut them into quarters. Mix them with the nori purée, adding a little of the potato cooking water if the purée needs loosening.

Put the John Dory on to a serving plate and pull off the skin so everyone can get at the soft white flesh. Serve the seaweed potatoes alongside.

Rib of beef with spring veg and anchovy butter

When you have good-quality beef it doesn't need much done to it. I like my food to be punchy, and the anchovy butter is exactly that.

SERVES 4

RIB OF BEEF
2kg rib of beef
sunflower oil
100g butter
1 garlic bulb, cut in half across
10g thyme
sea salt

SPRING VEG AND ANCHOVY BUTTER
50g tinned brown anchovy fillets, drained
150g softened butter
200g bunch of asparagus
200g purple sprouting broccoli
sunflower oil

Preheat your oven to 120°c fan.

Season the beef all over with about a tablespoon of sea salt. In a hot pan with a splash of sunflower oil, sear the beef for 8 to 10 minutes until it has a really good colour all over. Turn the heat down a little, then add the butter, the halved garlic bulb and the thyme. Let the butter melt, then use it to baste the beef for 2 minutes. Transfer the beef to a roasting tin and brush it all over with the melted butter, then put it in the oven. Cook for an hour, or until a meat thermometer reads 48°c, then rest for 30 minutes.

Finely chop the anchovies and mix them through the butter, or just blitz them together until smooth.

Snap the woody ends off the asparagus, then remove the leaves with a knife. Slice the asparagus in half lengthways. Cut the bulky stems off the broccoli. Blanch the veg in boiling, salted water for 1 minute and drain.

When you're ready to eat, pan fry the broccoli and asparagus with a little oil on a high heat until they are starting to brown. Warm the anchovy butter in a pot.

Carve the beef on to a big serving plate, then pile the charred broccoli and asparagus on another dish and pour over the anchovy butter.

Banana chocolate chip cookie

I love cookies. Marylands are the best for dipping in a cup of tea, giant Millie's Cookies for birthday celebrations, M & S's freshly baked milk chocolate chip paired with a glass of milk… I could go on!

So, I knew I had to put a cookie recipe in this book. It needed to be chewy, crispy, sweet and salty – a blend of all my favourites. I hope you enjoy it as much as I do.

Keep the chocolate in big pieces so that it doesn't completely melt into the mix – about the size of a ten pence piece. Buy chocolate in bars rather than bags of chips and chop it yourself; the better the quality of the chocolate, the better the cookie will be.

MAKES 15

175g bread flour
½ tsp baking powder
½ tsp bicarbonate of soda
½ tsp sea salt
75g caster sugar
125g dark soft brown sugar
115g unsalted butter, softened
1 medium egg
50g mashed banana
   (about half a banana)
75g milk chocolate,
   chopped into large pieces
75g dark chocolate,
   chopped into large pieces
30g white chocolate,
   chopped into large pieces
30g mini marshmallows

2 baking trays, lined with
   greaseproof paper

Sift the flour, baking powder, bicarbonate of soda and sea salt into a bowl. Cream the caster and dark brown sugars and butter together until the mix starts to look fluffy and lighter in colour. Beat in the egg until it is fully incorporated, then stir in the flour mix. Finally, beat in the mashed banana, then stir through the milk, dark and white chocolate pieces and the mini marshmallows until they are well mixed in. Place the dough in the fridge to rest for at least an hour.

Preheat your oven to 175°c fan. Weigh the cookie dough into 50g portions and roll into balls between your palms. Arrange the balls on your lined baking trays, leaving a good amount of space between them as they'll spread while cooking. Flatten the tops with your hand, then put in the oven to bake for 14 to 16 minutes.

Leave to cool on a wire rack.

Gooseberry and Earl Grey Swiss roll

Who doesn't love cake, cream and jam? This is incredibly light and moreish and a lovely way to enjoy gooseberries. Store any leftovers in an airtight container in the fridge.

SERVES 10–14

EARL GREY CHANTILLY
300ml double cream
20g icing sugar
1 tbsp loose leaf Earl Grey tea

GOOSEBERRY JAM
250g green gooseberries
200g jam sugar

MILK SPONGE
4 eggs
40g flour
10g cornflour
45ml vegetable oil
45ml milk
60g sugar

32.5 × 32.5cm Silikomart silicone roulade mould

First, make the Earl Grey Chantilly as it needs time to infuse and chill. Put the cream in a pot and warm over a medium heat until steaming. Stir in the sugar, then add the tea and leave to infuse for 20 minutes. Strain through a sieve and then put the tea-scented cream into the fridge, covered with cling film, for at least 2 hours. When it is very cold, whip to soft peaks.

For the gooseberry jam, put the gooseberries in a pot with the jam sugar. Bring to a boil over a medium-high heat and stir to make sure all the sugar has dissolved. Turn down to a medium heat and cook until the jam reaches 105°C. Remove from the heat and leave to cool.

Preheat your oven to 180°C fan.

Separate the eggs into two bowls. Sieve the flour and cornflour into a third bowl and mix with the oil, then add to the yolks along with the milk and whisk until well combined.

Whip the egg whites with an electric hand-held mixer or stand mixer. Gradually add the sugar, whipping between each addition, and once it's all added whip to somewhere between soft and stiff peaks.

With a spatula, fold the meringue mix into the yolk mix a third at a time. When it's well combined, scrape out into the mould and gently spread into the corners and edges so you have an even layer. I usually put the mould on an overturned large baking tray so it's easier to move into the oven. Bake for 10 minutes and leave to cool for another 5 minutes.

Carefully tease the sponge out of the mould on to a wire rack and lay a piece of greaseproof paper on top. Flip it over so the paper is on the bottom, and roll it up tightly so the paper is wrapped inside. Cover with a tea towel and set aside to cool.

Once the cake is completely cool, unroll it and discard the greaseproof, then spread with a layer of jam followed by a layer of Chantilly. Carefully roll the cake back up again and trim the ends for a really sharp finish. Move the Swiss roll on to your serving plate and put it into the fridge for an hour to firm up before you eat.

Strawberry and elderflower sundae

An ice cream sundae always makes me feel like a big kid – I love them! This recipe has a more grown-up feel to it, but bags of nostalgia too. The perfect way to celebrate the first Scottish strawberries.

SERVES 4

STRAWBERRY COMPOTE
400g strawberries
80g sugar
2 tsp strawberry vinegar (page 276) or white balsamic

ALMOND CRUNCH
50g flaked almonds, toasted (page 23)
30g almond butter
10g icing sugar
salt

ELDERFLOWER CHANTILLY
150ml fridge-cold double cream
40ml elderflower cordial (page 70 or if you're tight on time you can buy this from the supermarket)

TO SERVE
500g tub of shop-bought vanilla ice cream

4 sundae glasses

The strawberry compote is very simple to make but you need to start it the day before. Cut the strawberries into 2cm pieces and put them in a single layer on a tray in the freezer overnight. The next morning, once they are frozen solid, mix them with the sugar and leave to defrost at room temperature, stirring occasionally. Strain through a sieve set over a bowl and keep the juice. Add the vinegar to the juice, then taste and adjust – you don't need too much, just a splash to cut through the sweet flavours.

To make the almond crunch, put the toasted flaked almonds in a bowl with the almond butter, icing sugar and salt and combine (using your hands is easiest).

For the elderflower Chantilly, just mix the cream and the cordial together in a bowl and whip to soft peaks.

Build up the sundae in layers: first a spoonful of the strained strawberries, then a scoop or two of ice cream, then another layer of strawberries and a good drizzle of the juice. Repeat until you get to the top of the glass, then top with a pile of elderflower Chantilly and a handful of almond crunch.

Spring dinner party menu

Who doesn't love a dinner party? We've had many over the years that range from chilled relaxed evenings to drinking into the small hours and dancing on tables! They've all had one thing in common though – great food.

This spring dinner party menu features:

A selection of different starters – chilled langoustines, asparagus and bagna cauda, a rich sunflower seed dip with flatbreads – on the table to share.

Roasted lamb shoulder, potatoes and greens with black garlic mayo

---

And finishing up with a gorgeous rhubarb and orange pavlova.

Sake and elderflower fizz

Sake has a beautiful savouriness to it which works really well in long, refreshing drinks. The perfect foil to beautiful elderflower, with some fizz for extra luxury.

SERVES 1

35ml sake
25ml elderflower cordial
sparkling wine
ice

Build the cocktail in a tall glass. Pour the sake and elderflower cordial in first, then fill the glass with ice and top up with sparkling wine. Give it a little stir before you serve.

Elderflower cordial

This recipe will make more elderflower cordial than you need, but it'll keep for a few weeks bottled in the fridge and is delicious as a soft drink mixed with soda, or to make a strawberry and elderflower sundae (page 66).

MAKES 1.5 LITRES

500g sugar
20 elderflower heads
2 lemons, thinly sliced
2 oranges, thinly sliced
2 tbsp citric acid

In a large pan, bring a litre of water to the boil. Add the sugar and mix until dissolved. Leave to cool.

Wash the elderflower heads in cold water and drain, then add them to the cool syrup with the lemon, orange and citric acid. Make sure everything is submerged and infuse for 24 hours.

Strain through a muslin cloth and store in a bottle or Kilner jar in the fridge.

Spring dinner party starters

I love having a selection of different dishes on the table to share with friends – it's my favourite way to eat and the perfect way to start off a dinner party. Everything here can be made in the morning and finished at the last minute.

Sunflower seed dip

SERVES 6

200g sunflower seeds
175g sunflower oil
2 garlic cloves, roughly chopped
4 tsp white wine vinegar
1 tsp fine salt
juice and zest of ½ lemon

Place 190g of the sunflower seeds and the oil in a pot and bring up to a medium heat. Gently toast the seeds in the bubbling oil for about 10 to 15 mins, until they are a pale golden brown – they will keep browning as they cool in the oil. Leave to cool.

Put the seeds with their cooking oil into a blender and add the garlic, vinegar, salt and 225ml water. Blitz until smooth and silky – this will take up to 10 minutes – then scrape out into a bowl. Add the lemon juice and zest and mix through, then taste and season with more salt if needed. Toast the remaining sunflower seeds in a dry pan until golden and scatter them over the top.

Asparagus bagna cauda

SERVES 6

BAGNA CAUDA
6 garlic cloves
100ml olive oil
50g tinned brown anchovies
100ml milk
1 tbsp white wine vinegar

12 asparagus spears

Thinly slice the garlic and sweat in a pot with a splash of the olive oil until softened. Add in the anchovies and milk and simmer gently for 10 minutes.

Transfer to a blender and, whilst blending, gradually pour in the remaining oil until everything has emulsified. Finish with the white wine vinegar, then taste and adjust if necessary.

Using a small knife, remove the leaves from the asparagus spears. Snap off the woody ends, then blanch the asparagus in boiling, salted water for 2 minutes.

Drain the asparagus and transfer to a serving bowl, then generously drizzle with bagna cauda.

Flatbreads

MAKES 12

225g strong bread flour
7g sachet instant dried yeast
1 tsp sea salt
1 tsp sugar
110g yoghurt
sunflower/vegetable oil

Put the flour, yeast and salt in a mixing bowl. In a small saucepan, warm the sugar and yoghurt with 110ml water to about body temperature – you don't want it to get too hot as it will kill the yeast. Add to the flour and mix until you have a smooth dough.

Transfer the dough to an oiled bowl and cover with cling film. Leave at room temperature for an hour until it has doubled in size.

Knock back the dough and turn out on a lightly floured work surface. Divide it into twelve portions of 30g each and roll them into balls. Line a deep tray with greaseproof paper that has been brushed with sunflower oil, and spread out the dough balls on the tray with enough space for them to double in size. Cover with cling film and leave to prove at room temperature for 30 minutes. Once proved, you can either cook them immediately or pop them in the fridge until needed.

To shape the flatbreads, first rub a little oil on your hands to prevent sticking and make it easier to handle the dough. Gently press and stretch a dough ball between your palms, aiming for a nice round shape about 10cm in diameter.

In a griddle or frying pan, add enough oil to cover the base and put over a medium heat. Place in as many flatbreads as can comfortably fit and cook them for 2 minutes on each side, until they are nice and golden.

Serve immediately or leave them to cool on a wire rack and, when you're ready to eat, reheat in your oven for 2 to 3 minutes at 170°c fan. Splash a small amount of water in your oven to create a little steam when you put them in.

Langoustines with wild garlic mayonnaise

I make this bright green mayo with wild garlic oil. However, if you're pushed for time you can blitz blanched wild garlic leaves with shop-bought or home-made mayo and it will still be delicious.

SERVES 6

12 large live langoustines
1 tbsp salt

WILD GARLIC MAYONNAISE
150g wild garlic
200ml sunflower oil
2 egg yolks
2 tbsp Dijon mustard
1 tsp white wine vinegar
1 tsp fine salt

Using a tea towel to hold the langoustine steady, carefully pierce each one in the head with the tip of a small, sharp knife, making sure you go all the way through.

Fill a large, deep pot with water and bring to a rapid boil, then add the salt. Blanch the langoustines, six at a time, for 30 seconds then lift them out of the water and let them cool down to room temperature. If you're cooking them more than 30 minutes in advance, pop them in the fridge.

Next make some wild garlic oil for the mayonnaise. Cut the stems off the wild garlic and put the leaves into a blender with the sunflower oil. Blitz for 5 minutes, then transfer to a pot over a medium heat. Stirring continuously, bring it up to 80°c, then strain through a muslin into a jug and leave to cool.

Put the egg yolks, mustard, vinegar and salt in a small bowl and mix together. Slowly add 100ml of the wild garlic oil, whisking all the time, until you have a lovely thick, green mayonnaise.

Alternatively, you can just blanch the wild garlic leaves in boiling, salted water for 10 seconds and refresh in ice water. Once cold, drain them and squeeze out any excess water. Put the blanched wild garlic into a blender with 160ml mayonnaise and blitz until smooth. Taste and adjust the seasoning if necessary.

Crack the claws of the langoustines, then pile them on a plate and serve with the wild garlic mayonnaise on the side.

Slow roast lamb shoulder and lamb fat potatoes

One of my favourite parts of this dish is the potatoes – they taste incredible cooked in the fat that's dripped from the shoulder!

SERVES 6

LAMB SHOULDER
1.5kg lamb shoulder (bone in)
2 tbsp sunflower oil
1 tbsp cumin seeds
1 tbsp fennel seeds
1 tbsp sea salt
3 celery sticks, roughly chopped
4 carrots, peeled and roughly chopped
1 onion, roughly chopped
4 bay leaves
10g thyme
1 garlic bulb

LAMB FAT POTATOES
1.5kg Maris Piper potatoes
1 tbsp fine salt

BLACK GARLIC YOGHURT
50g black garlic paste
200g yoghurt
a pinch of salt

CHARRED GREENS
150g green beans, trimmed
150g sugar snaps
1 tsp sunflower oil
40g wild garlic
40g wild leeks
1 tsp lemon juice
1 tbsp olive oil
salt

Preheat your oven to 165°c fan.

Drizzle the lamb with the sunflower oil, then sprinkle the cumin and fennel seeds and sea salt all over it.

Place the chopped celery, carrots and onion in the bottom of a roasting tray with the bay leaves and thyme. Cut the garlic bulb in half across and add it to the veg, then pop the lamb shoulder on top and cover with tin foil. Cook for 2½ hours, then take off the tin foil and cook for another hour, until the meat is tender and falling off the bone.

Whilst the lamb is cooking you can organise your potatoes. Peel and cut them to whatever size you like your roasties. Place them in a pot, cover with cold water and add the tablespoon of fine salt. Bring them to the boil over a medium heat and cook for 10 minutes, until the outside is cooked but they're still a little hard in the middle. Drain off the water and put them back in the pot, put the lid on and shake them around so they get a little bashed.

Take the lamb out of the roasting tin and set it aside to rest. Turn the oven up to 200°c fan. Use a slotted spoon to remove the veg from the roasting tin, leaving behind as much of the fat that has dripped out of the lamb as you can. Put the tin back in the oven for 5 minutes to get the fat nice and hot, then carefully add the parboiled potatoes and roll them around so they're covered in fat. Roast the potatoes for 30 minutes, until golden and crispy, turning them every 10 minutes or so.

Mix the black garlic paste, yoghurt and salt together. Taste and add more salt if required, then set aside at room temperature.

Recipe continues overleaf

Just before you're ready to eat, do the charred greens. Fill a pot with water and enough salt that it tastes like the sea and bring to a boil. Blanch the green beans and sugar snaps for 3 minutes, then drain and pat the vegetables dry. In a large frying pan, heat the sunflower oil so it's hot, then add the sugar snaps and green beans and sauté for 30 seconds. Add in the wild garlic and wild leeks and cook for another 30 seconds, keeping the pan moving, until they've wilted down. Mix the lemon juice and olive oil together and dress the greens.

Put the potatoes on to your serving dish and place the lamb shoulder on top, then scatter the dressed greens around the edges.

Rhubarb and orange pavlova

This recipe is from a good friend and old colleague of mine from my Castle Terrace days. It's actually his mum's recipe and they're from New Zealand, where they take the pavlova very seriously, so as you can imagine it's bloody good. (It's also very specific!)

Older eggs are better for pavlova, and they MUST be at room temperature. Use the shells to separate out the whites and keep the yolks for mayonnaise (page 280).

SERVES 6–8

PAVLOVA

6 egg whites at room temperature
400g caster sugar
1 tsp vanilla paste
1 tsp malt vinegar
2 tbsp cornflour

RHUBARB AND ORANGE TOPPING

350g rhubarb, trimmed and cut into 1cm slices
80g sugar
20g dried hibiscus
3 oranges
1 recipe roasted vanilla cream (see opposite)

Preheat your oven to 120°C fan. Line a tray with greaseproof paper.

In a stand mixer or with an electric handheld mixer on medium speed, whisk the egg whites to soft peaks. Start adding the caster sugar a teaspoon at a time: it needs to be added very slowly and the whole process should take 10 minutes.

Turn off the mixer and add the vanilla paste, vinegar and cornflour, then mix for another minute. Use a little of the mix to stick the greaseproof paper to the baking tray at each corner to stop it from blowing on to the pavlova whilst its cooking. Dollop the rest of the mix on to the lined baking tray, spreading it with a spatula so to form a neat circle about 20cm in diameter. (You can draw a 20cm circle on the underside of your paper if you'd like a guide.) Use upward strokes of the spatula to build up the sides.

Place the pavlova in your oven on the middle shelf and cook for 1½ hours without opening the door to check it. When the time is up, turn the oven off but still don't open the door, and leave it to cool completely, about 4 hours or overnight. Meanwhile, you can get on with making the roasted vanilla cream.

Once the pavlova is completely cold, use a large palette knife to remove the greaseproof paper and transfer it to your serving plate.

Put the sliced rhubarb and sugar into a heatproof bowl. Tie the hibiscus in a bit of muslin and add to the bowl, then cover it with cling film. Put the bowl over a pot of simmering water for 10 minutes, until the sugar has melted and the rhubarb has just softened. Take the bowl off the heat and set it aside to cool, then squeeze any juice out of the hibiscus in its muslin before you discard it.

Using a small, sharp, serrated knife, cut the skin off the oranges, making sure there's no pith left. Cut out the individual segments, holding each orange over a bowl to catch all the juice, and discard any pips or bits of membrane. Squeeze any last bits of juice from the leftovers, then put the segments into the juice until you need them.

Spread the roasted vanilla cream over the top of the pavlova. Decorate with the sliced rhubarb and orange segments.

Roasted vanilla cream

This is super simple but you do need to leave it to infuse and chill for 2½ hours before whipping.

MAKES 250ML

4 vanilla pods
250ml double cream

Preheat your oven to 170°c fan. Put the vanilla pods on a tray and roast them in the oven for 15 minutes, until they are nice and crispy. Using a small knife, cut the pods in half lengthways, then use the side of the knife to scrape out the seeds.

Place the cream into a pot and add the vanilla seeds and scraped pods. Heat until the cream is steaming but not boiling, then take the pot off the boil and leave to infuse for 30 minutes. Strain through a sieve, then put in the fridge to chill for at least 2 hours. Whip to soft peaks.

Summer

Ripe, juicy tomatoes, Scottish shellfish, berries, stone fruits, barbecues and drinking fizz in the garden – all the things I love and long for in the build-up to summer.

Oysters with tomato and celery

A really clean and flavoursome accompaniment to an oyster.

SERVES 4

450g vine tomatoes
1 tsp fine salt
1 celery stick
8 oysters, shucked (page 10)
extra virgin olive oil

Blanch two of the tomatoes in boiling water for 10 seconds, then refresh them in a bowl of iced water. Peel off the skin, then cut them into quarters and set the seeds aside (but don't throw them away). Trim the core and any hard bits (again, don't throw these away), then cut the flesh into 5mm dice and put them in a bowl in the fridge.

Roughly chop the remaining tomatoes and put into a blender with the salt and the reserved tomato seeds and trim. Blend until you have a pulpy purée. Line a colander with muslin and set over a bowl, then pour in the tomato mixture and leave it to drip through for at least 2 hours. Once all the tomato water has dripped through, put it into the fridge to chill and discard the pulp.

Peel the celery stick and cut into 5mm dice, then mix with the tomato dice.

Taste your tomato water and adjust the seasoning if necessary.

Spoon some of the tomato and celery dice on to your open oysters. Pour in enough tomato water to cover the oyster, and finish with a few drops of extra virgin olive oil.

Tomatoes and tapenade on toast

A classic combination that's never going to go out of fashion, this is a lovely way to celebrate heritage tomatoes when they are at their best.

SERVES 4

1kg heritage tomatoes
2 tbsp red wine vinegar
2 tbsp extra virgin olive oil
1 tsp sea salt
100g tinned brown anchovies
4 slices of sourdough
1 tbsp sunflower oil

TAPENADE
2 anchovy fillets
150g pitted black olives
½ garlic clove
2 tbsp capers (well rinsed if salted)
2 tbsp extra virgin olive oil
juice of ½ lemon

Cut the tomatoes into wedges or thick slices and put into a bowl. Drizzle with the red wine vinegar and 2 tablespoons of olive oil, then sprinkle over the sea salt and leave for about 20 minutes to come up to room temperature.

To make the tapenade, take a couple of your tinned anchovies and put them in a blender with the olives, garlic, capers, olive oil and lemon juice. Blitz until you have a smooth paste.

Drizzle the sourdough slices with sunflower oil and chargrill until nicely toasted. Allow to cool a little, then spread over a good layer of tapenade. Pile each slice with tomatoes and finish with the rest of your anchovies.

Chicken liver parfait and peaches on toast

This is a delicious dish to have as a starter or snack: the sweetness of the peach is so good with the rich parfait. I'd suggest making the parfait the day before as it needs time to cool and set. The top layer of the parfait will oxidise, so the best thing to do is to scrape it off before you serve it and use all the delicious parfait underneath.

SERVES 4

CHICKEN LIVER PARFAIT
1 shallot, thinly sliced
130ml brandy
130ml port
40g butter
40g duck fat
150g chicken livers
1 tsp salt
2 egg yolks
150ml double cream

TO SERVE
4 slices of focaccia (page 92)
2 peaches, sliced
micro cress

The day before, start on your parfait. Preheat your oven to 120°C fan.

Place the thinly sliced shallot in a pot with the brandy and port, and reduce until almost dry. Allow to cool.

Gently melt the butter and duck fat and allow to cool slightly.

Prepare the chicken livers, removing any sinew. Put them in a blender with the shallots and salt and blitz until smooth. While the blender is running, add in the egg yolks, then the cream, then the melted and cooled butter and duck fat. Blend for 5 to 10 seconds – just enough to emulsify the ingredients together. Pass the mixture through a fine sieve and pour into a ceramic terrine mould or a loaf tin.

Cover the mould with tin foil, then place it into a deep baking tray. Pour some hot water into the tray so it comes halfway up the mould, and cook in the oven for about an hour. You want the parfait to be almost set, with a slight jiggle.

Remove the parfait from the bain-marie and allow to cool completely. Place it in the fridge to set, covered with cling film. The next day, scrape off the top layer if it's oxidised, then spoon it into a piping bag, if you're using one.

When you're ready to eat, chargrill or toast the focaccia. Just before serving, cut the tip off the piping bag at an angle so you'll get a nice ribbony texture, and pipe the parfait on to the focaccia (or you can just spread it on). Scatter with peach slices and finish with a few of the herbs.

Focaccia

This wonderful recipe comes from Kip Preidys, who also gave me the pasta dough recipe on page 281. The key to getting it right is to treat it like you would a sourdough: add the water to the dough gradually as you knead it and allow plenty of time for it to prove.

MAKES 1 LARGE FOCACCIA

500g strong flour
7g (1 sachet) instant dried yeast
2 tsp sugar
2 tsp salt
olive oil
sea salt

20 × 20cm baking tin, lined with greaseproof paper

Preheat your oven to 200°c fan.

In a stand mixer with the dough hook fitted (or in a large bowl), mix together the flour, yeast, sugar and salt.

Add 250ml warm water and mix until fully incorporated, then mix for 20 minutes, adding another 150ml water splash by splash so it's mixed in gradually. Add 2 teaspoons of olive oil and mix until fully incorporated.

Transfer the dough to an oiled container. After 30 minutes, stretch and fold the dough with wet hands: just lift the dough from underneath, letting each side flop down, then put it back down with the ends tucked underneath. Leave for another 30 minutes and repeat.

After another 30 minutes, place the dough into your lined baking tin and cover with cling film. Let it rest and spread in the tray for 30 minutes.

With wet hands, gently stretch the dough to the edges of the baking tin and poke indents into the dough with your fingers. Sprinkle with sea salt and leave for a final 30 minutes.

Preheat your oven to 200°c fan.

Drizzle 1½ tablespoons of olive oil over the dough, then put it into the oven to bake for 25 to 30 minutes, until nicely risen and golden brown with a good crust. Allow the focaccia to cool a little in the tin before turning it out on to a wire rack.

Basil panisse

Bougie crisps and dip!!

SERVES 4

PANISSE
½ tbsp olive oil
1 tsp salt
180g gram/chickpea flour, sieved
60g Parmesan cheese, finely grated
5g basil, roughly chopped

SOUR CREAM DIP
150ml sour cream
150ml mayonnaise
10g chives, finely chopped
salt

vegetable oil for deep-frying

18 × 18cm container, lined with cling film

The panisse mix thickens very quickly, so it's important to have your container lined and everything sieved, grated and chopped before you start.

Put 400ml water in a shallow, wide-based pan, then add the olive oil and salt. Place on a medium-high heat and bring to a boil. Add in the sieved gram flour and cook, whisking continuously, for about 5 minutes, until you have a very thick paste that comes away from the sides of the pan. Mix in the Parmesan until it is melted, then take the pan off the heat and stir through the basil.

Working quickly, scrape the panisse into your lined container and spread it into an even layer about 2cm thick. If the mix has set, use a wet spatula to help you spread it. Leave to cool, then put the tray in the fridge for at least 45 minutes.

While the panisse is chilling, make your dip: simply mix together the sour cream, mayo and chives and add a pinch of salt to taste.

Once the panisse has completely chilled and set, cut it into chunky chips about 9cm long and 2cm wide. Heat about 5cm vegetable oil in a deep pan and bring up to 180°C, then fry the panisse in batches until crispy and golden brown all over. Drain on kitchen roll and serve with the sour cream dip.

Tomato and watermelon salad

Tasty, fresh and sweet – everything you want in a summer salad.

SERVES 4

DRESSING
150g vine tomatoes, roughly chopped
180g watermelon, peeled and roughly chopped
2 tbsp white balsamic vinegar
1 tsp sea salt

SALAD
600g heritage tomatoes, cut into 4cm pieces
1 tbsp red wine vinegar
1 tbsp extra virgin olive oil
1 tsp sea salt
250g watermelon, peeled and cut into 4cm pieces
a handful of micro herbs and flowers

First, make the dressing. Put the chopped vine tomatoes and watermelon into a blender and blitz until smooth. Pass through a sieve into a bowl (discarding the pulp left in the sieve) then add the white balsamic and salt. Taste and adjust the seasoning if needed. Chill for an hour.

To make the salad, put the tomatoes into a bowl and drizzle with the red wine vinegar, oil and sea salt. Put the watermelon in another bowl, then set both aside for at least 20 minutes to come to room temperature.

Lay the tomatoes and watermelon on your plates, then spoon over the dressing and finish with the herbs and flowers.

Sunflower seed gazpacho and grilled peaches

This is a great dish for when you're entertaining – it can be scaled up easily and the flavour only gets better as it tempers out of the fridge. You can use any bread you like in the gazpacho, including gluten-free.

SERVES 4

SUNFLOWER SEED GAZPACHO
130g sunflower seeds, toasted
25g bread, roughly chopped
¼ cucumber, peeled and roughly chopped
½ garlic clove, thinly sliced
400ml oat milk (or dairy milk, but oat milk keeps it vegan!)
4 tsp sherry vinegar
1 tsp olive oil
1 tsp salt
a pinch of ground pepper

TO FINISH
6 peaches, halved and stoned
16 small courgettes with their flowers
olive oil
fine salt

The first thing to do is make the sunflower seed gazpacho. In a bowl, mix 110g of the sunflower seeds with the bread, cucumber and garlic. Add the oat milk, sherry vinegar, olive oil, salt and pepper and mix thoroughly, then leave to marinate for a minimum of 2 hours and a maximum of 24. If you're leaving it for longer than a few hours, put it into the fridge. Blend the gazpacho until smooth, check the seasoning and adjust to taste. If it has been marinating in the fridge, let it come up to room temperature before blending.

When you're nearly ready to eat, you can prep everything else. Cut each peach half into four wedges, then lightly salt them and rub very lightly with some oil. Place on a hot griddle or barbecue that has burnt down to white coals, and cook the peaches for a few minutes until they are slightly soft and have taken on some of the char.

Next, carefully separate the flowers from the courgettes and lightly season them with salt.

Slice the courgettes lengthways, season with salt, and drizzle with a little olive oil. Put them on the barbecue or griddle and cook for 2 to 3 minutes on each side until just tender.

Now that everything is ready you can start to plate up. Randomly arrange the peaches and courgettes on the plate, then drizzle generously with the sunflower seed gazpacho. Gently tear the courgette flowers into petals and scatter them around the plate. Finally, roughly chop the reserved toasted sunflower seeds and sprinkle over the top.

Ricotta-stuffed courgette flowers with romesco

Romesco is the perfect accompaniment to beautiful courgette flowers. It's traditionally made with almonds but can be made with any nuts. I really like using smoked almonds – the salty smokiness adds interesting depth and layers. Roast the peppers for the romesco at the same time as you roast the garlic for the courgette flower stuffing – they take the same amount of time but the peppers will need to be turned halfway through.

SERVES 4

1 garlic bulb
300g ricotta
zest of 1 lemon
4 courgettes with their flowers

TEMPURA
80g rice flour
120g cornflour
160ml chilled sparkling water
fine salt

1l sunflower oil for deep-frying

Preheat the oven to 170°c fan.

Wrap the garlic loosely in tin foil and roast in the oven for about 30 minutes, until the garlic is soft. Allow it to cool, then squeeze each soft clove out of its skin into a bowl. Beat with a spoon until you have a smooth paste, then add in the ricotta and lemon zest and mix thoroughly.

Put the ricotta stuffing in a piping bag and fill the courgette flowers until they are almost full (you could also do this using a spoon). Set aside while you make the tempura batter.

In a large bowl, mix the rice flour and cornflour with a pinch of salt. Gradually add the sparkling water until you have a smooth but not-too-wet batter.

Pour the sunflower oil into a tall pot approximately 20cm in diameter and 20cm in height so it comes no more than a third of the way up the pot. Take it to a temperature of 175°c over a medium heat.

Place the courgette flowers (still connected to their courgettes) in the batter and, using your hands, make sure they are fully coated.

Carefully place the battered courgette flowers in the oil, two at a time, and fry for 3 minutes until they are golden brown, turning halfway through. Carefully remove from the oil with a slotted spoon and drain on a paper towel. Serve with lashings of romesco sauce!

Romesco sauce

You can keep any leftovers in the fridge in a jar for a few days.

MAKES ABOUT 500ML

4 red peppers
50g smoked almonds
50ml olive oil
1 garlic clove
1 tsp smoked paprika
2 tsp sherry vinegar
salt

Preheat the oven to 170°c fan.

Put the red peppers in a deep baking tray covered with tin foil and roast for about 30 minutes, turning them after 15 minutes.

Carefully transfer the roasted peppers to a bowl (they'll be hot and will have pepper juices inside them). Cover the bowl with cling film and set aside for 30 minutes – this makes it easier to remove the skin. Then peel off the skin and discard the seeds and any juices.

Place the peppers in a blender with the smoked almonds, olive oil, garlic, smoked paprika and sherry vinegar. Pulse a few times so you get a rough, textured sauce (you can blend it for longer if you would like it to be smoother). Season to taste.

Fresh cheese, tomato and courgette tarts

This dish has maximum reward for a fairly minimal amount of effort. It's delicious to eat and you'll get a real sense of achievement when you realise how easy it is to make fresh cheese.

SERVES 4

½ recipe cream cheese pastry, rested (page 281)
4 heritage tomatoes, cut into pieces
1 courgette, very thinly sliced
1 recipe fresh cheese (page 280)
sea salt

TOMATO DRESSING

350g vine tomatoes
½ tsp salt
½ tsp white wine vinegar
½ tbsp cold-pressed rapeseed oil

four 8cm tart tins with removable bases

On a floured worktop, roll the pastry to 5mm thick and cut into four circles big enough to line your tart tins. Carefully press the pastry into the cases and put them in the fridge to rest for 30 minutes.

Preheat your oven to 175°c fan. Line the pastry with a double layer of cling film, making sure there is excess to go over the edges. Fill with ceramic baking beans – I prefer to use ceramic beans as they hold the heat and cook the pastry more evenly.

Bake the tart cases for 15 minutes, then check, gently lifting one side of cling film to see if the pastry is completely cooked and starting to colour. If they're still a little undercooked, give them a few more minutes. Remove the beans and place the tart cases back in the oven until the pastry is golden brown all over. Leave to cool, then remove from the tins.

To make the dressing, blend the vine tomatoes with the salt. Line a sieve with a muslin cloth and put it over a bowl, then pour in the tomatoes. Don't press or squeeze the tomatoes, just let the tomato water drip through – it will take anywhere from 30 minutes to an hour.

Add the vinegar and rapeseed oil to the tomato water, and whisk the dressing together.

Put the tomato chunks into a bowl and let them come to room temperature, then season with a little salt and pour over the dressing. Leave them to sit for 5 minutes.

Lightly season the sliced courgette with sea salt.

Half fill the tart cases with the fresh cheese, then build up the tarts with tomatoes and slices of courgette. Add another tablespoon of the dressing from the tomato bowl to each tart just before serving.

Lobster rolls

An absolute classic!

SERVES 4

MILK ROLLS
160g strong flour
80ml whole milk
1½ tsp milk powder
25g sugar
½ tsp salt
3.5g (½ sachet) instant dried yeast
1 egg, beaten
40g softened butter
2 egg yolks for glazing

ROCKET MAYONNAISE
1 recipe mayonnaise (page 280)
   or 160ml Hellmann's
50g rocket
juice of ½ lemon

TO SERVE
1 baby gem lettuce
250g butter
meat from 2 cooked lobsters
   (page 12)
4 lemon wedges

Begin with the rolls. In a small pot, mix 10g of the flour and 20ml of the milk with 20ml water and cook, stirring continuously, over a medium-low heat until it thickens to a stiff paste. Allow to cool. This is your starter dough.

In a stand mixer with the dough hook fitted, mix the remaining 150g flour with the milk powder, sugar, salt and yeast. Add the rest of the milk (60ml), the beaten egg and the starter dough and mix until fully incorporated, then add in the softened butter and mix on a low speed for 5 minutes (or knead by hand if you're not using a mixer). Transfer the dough to an oiled bowl and cover with cling film. Leave to prove at room temperature for about 2 hours, until the dough has doubled in size.

Knock back the proved milk bun dough and turn it out on to a floured worktop. Divide into four portions, then shape each one into a sub. Place on to a deep greaseproof-lined tray and cover with cling film, then leave for an hour until they are nice and puffy.

Preheat your oven to 180°c fan. Carefully brush the milk buns with the beaten egg yolk and bake for 10 minutes, then transfer to a wire rack to cool.

To make the rocket mayonnaise, put the mayo in a blender with the rocket and blitz until it is fully combined. Finish with a splash of lemon juice to taste.

Cut the root off the baby gem and peel off the leaves, then wash and spin them dry.

When you're ready to eat, melt the butter in a pot. Cut the lobster into smaller pieces. Take the butter off the heat, add the lobster meat so it's all submerged and leave it to soak up the butter for 2 minutes.

Slice the milk buns lengthways but not all the way through so they open up, and spread a generous layer of rocket mayonnaise on both sides. Add a couple of lettuce leaves, then pile in pieces of lobster meat and drizzle with a little of the butter. Serve with a wedge of lemon.

Pork belly B.L.T.

Perfect at any time of day – breakfast, lunch, dinner! For best results you need to brine your pork belly in a 5% brine for 12 hours before cooking it.

SERVES 4

PORK BELLY
100g salt
1kg boneless pork belly
4 carrots, peeled and roughly chopped
2 celery sticks, roughly chopped
1 onion, roughly chopped
10g thyme
1 garlic bulb, cut in half across
100ml maple syrup
sunflower oil

30g black garlic paste
100g mayonnaise (page 280)
100g baby tomatoes, halved
1 tbsp white wine vinegar
1 tbsp cold-pressed rapeseed oil
1 foccacia (page 92)
1 baby gem lettuce
sea salt

The day before you want to cook, make a 5% brine for the pork belly: warm 200ml water in a pot and add the salt, stirring until it has dissolved, then add another 1.8l water. Put the pork belly into a large container and pour over the brine, making sure the meat is fully submerged. Put into the fridge for 12 hours.

The next day, preheat your oven to 140°c fan. Put the chopped carrots, celery and onion into a roasting tin with the thyme and halved bulb of garlic, then drain the pork belly and put it on top. Cover with tin foil and cook for 4 hours until the meat is tender. Put the meat on to a tray, then cover it with a board and put a weight on the top. Leave to cool, then cut into eight fat slices.

Mix the black garlic paste and mayo together and set aside. Sprinkle the halved tomatoes with a little sea salt, then drizzle with the white wine vinegar and cold-pressed rapeseed oil. Leave at room temperature for 20 minutes.

Trim the focaccia to a 20 × 20cm square, then cut it in half horizontally as if you were making a huge sandwich. Generously spread each cut side with the black garlic mayonnaise.

Place the pork belly slices in a warm pan with a little sunflower oil and pan fry over a medium-high heat until crispy, about 2 minutes on each side. Add the maple syrup into the pan and cook for another 30 seconds, basting the pork with the syrup.

On the focaccia base, layer up the baby gem, then the tomatoes, then the pork belly slices. Put the top of the focaccia on, then cut into quarters and serve.

Grouse and tattie scones

The Glorious Twelfth marks the start of the shooting season, and grouse is the first game that you're allowed to shoot. It's always a race to get the birds back to the restaurant from the shoot, plucked, gutted and prepped in time for dinner service. I have memories of services when we've had orders of grouse on but they're still not in the building – stressful but fun! It's my favourite of all the game, and this is a very non-traditional way of serving it.

Use whatever mushrooms you're able to get here – cultivated mushrooms are fine if that's what you've got.

SERVES 4

TATTIE SCONE
400g Maris Piper potatoes
50g butter
1 egg
80g plain flour
1 tsp salt
1 tsp baking powder
1 tsp oil

8 grouse breasts, skin on if possible
sunflower oil
100g butter
3 garlic cloves, finely chopped
20g parsley, finely chopped
400g wild mushrooms, cut into big pieces about 3 × 10cm
50g ceps, thinly sliced
fine salt

Make the tattie scones first. Preheat the oven to 175°c fan. Pierce the potatoes with a fork and place them on a tray, then bake in the oven for 45 minutes to 1 hour until cooked through and tender. Once cooked, cut the potatoes in half and scoop out the flesh, then pass the flesh through a sieve or ricer. Add the butter and egg to the potato mash and gently mix through. In another bowl, mix together the flour, salt and baking powder. Slowly beat this into the potatoes – don't add it all at once as the dough will become gloopy. Divide into eight balls and mould each one into a flat, round pancake about 10cm wide and 1cm thick. Warm the oil in a frying pan over a medium heat and then pan fry the tattie scones for 2 minutes on each side. Place them to one side to cool, then pop them in the fridge for 30 minutes to firm up.

Season the grouse breasts all over with some fine salt. Heat a tablespoon of oil in a large frying pan over a medium-high heat, then place the grouse in skin-side down and cook for 1 minute. Carefully turn the grouse breasts over and put half of the butter into the pan. Once it has melted and started to foam, use it to baste the meat for 1 minute. Take the grouse out of the pan and leave it to rest for 5 minutes.

In a small bowl, mix the chopped garlic and parsley. Wipe the grouse pan out with kitchen roll, then pour in another tablespoon of oil and set it on a medium-high heat. Add in the wild mushrooms and cook for 3 minutes or so until they have a bit of colour, then add the remaining 50g butter and let it melt. Stir the chopped garlic and parsley mix through and cook for a minute more, being careful not to let the garlic burn.

Reheat the tattie scones in a dry pan and place two on each plate. Discard the skin from the grouse and carve the meat into thick slices. Place some garlicky mushrooms on the tattie scones, then arrange a few grouse slices on top. Garnish with some very thinly sliced raw ceps.

Watercress gnudi

Gnudi are just as delicious as gnocchi but take half the time to make. Paired with the velvety pine nut sauce, they make a really decadent dinner.

SERVES 2

PINE NUT SAUCE
125g pine nuts
200ml milk
½ tsp salt
1 tbsp cold-pressed rapeseed oil

WATERCRESS GNUDI
200g ricotta
1 egg
40g panko breadcrumbs
30g Parmesan, finely grated
10g watercress, leaves picked and finely chopped
zest of ½ lemon
1 tsp salt
sunflower oil

TO SERVE
sunflower oil
250g purple sprouting broccoli, trimmed into florets
50g pine nuts, toasted
zest of ½ lemon
Parmesan, grated
50g watercress, picked

Preheat your oven to 170°c fan. Pop the pine nuts on a heatproof tray and bake for 10 to 15 minutes until golden brown. Transfer the rest to a heatproof bowl, add the milk and salt and cover with cling film. Place over a pot of simmering water for 1 hour.

Transfer to a blender and gradually add the oil whilst blending. Blitz until smooth. Taste and adjust the seasoning if needed, then put it into a bowl with a piece of cling film pressed to the surface to prevent a skin forming.

For the gnudi, whisk the ricotta with the egg in a bowl, then beat in the breadcrumbs, Parmesan, watercress, lemon zest and salt.

Bring a pan of salted water to the boil. Meanwhile, take heaped teaspoons of the gnudi mixture and lightly roll them into fat little pillows. If the mixture feels too sticky, put a little flour on your hands. Put the finished gnudi on to a chopping board.

Once the water is boiling, tip the gnudi into the pan using a ladle and some of the boiling water to move them off the board.

Blanch in the salted simmering water for 3 minutes. When they float to the surface, use a slotted spoon to scoop them out, then let them dry out for about 30 minutes in a colander with a little splash of oil to coat them. Using the same pot and water, blanch the purple sprouting broccoli for 30 seconds and drain.

When you're ready to eat, put a little oil in a wide pan over a medium heat. Fry the gnudi until they're golden brown on each side, then take them out of the pan and set them aside. Add the broccoli to the pan, then increase the heat and get a nice char – about 2 minutes on each side.

Spread a generous layer of pine nut sauce on each plate, then arrange the gnudi and broccoli on top. Finish with a sprinkling of toasted pine nuts, lemon zest, Parmesan and a few watercress leaves.

Barbecued octopus and tomatoes

If I see octopus on a menu, I always order it – it's one of my favourite foods, and for me nothing says 'summer' more than octopus paired with tomatoes and lovage. It instantly transports me to the pintxos bars in San Sebastian – food heaven!

SERVES 4

1 octopus weighing about 2kg
4 heritage tomatoes
2½ tbsp olive oil
2½ tbsp red wine vinegar
100g lovage
100ml mayonnaise (page 280)
40g baby leaves
salt

Preheat your oven to 160°c fan.

Place the octopus in a deep tray and cover with tin foil. Place in the oven for 1 hour, then turn the octopus over, put the foil back on and cook for another hour. Allow the octopus to cool, then cut off the tentacles and discard everything else.

Slice the tomatoes and drizzle with half of the olive oil and half of the vinegar. Season with a little salt and set aside, allowing enough time for them to come up to room temperature.

If you're cooking the octopus on a barbecue, make sure that the flames have died down and the coals are white. Otherwise, heat up a griddle pan so it is nice and hot. Brush the octopus tentacles very lightly with oil, then either barbecue or sear them for about 2 minutes on each side, until nicely charred all over.

Blanch the lovage for 30 seconds in boiling water, then refresh in ice water. Squeeze out any excess moisture and put in a blender with the mayonnaise, then blitz until smooth and bright green.

Dress the baby leaves with the remaining olive oil and red wine vinegar and a little sea salt.

Place some slices of tomato and a few baby leaves on each plate, then put two octopus tentacles on top. Add a good dollop of lovage mayonnaise.

Bowl of clams, ham and peas

Ham hocks are a great ingredient: they're easy to cook and very reasonably priced, and the stock that you get from cooking them is incredible. With the addition of clams, it's heaven.

You need to rinse the clams a couple of times in cold water to remove any sand.

SERVES 4

1 smoked ham hock
1 onion, roughly chopped
1 leek, roughly chopped
3 bay leaves
10g thyme
2kg clams
240g fresh peas in the pod (120g podded weight)
100g butter, diced

Place the ham in a pot and cover with water. Bring to the boil, then strain and cover the ham with at least 2 litres of fresh water. Bring to a simmer, skim and add in the onion, leek, bay leaves and thyme. Simmer with the lid on until the ham is cooked and tender, about 4 hours.

With two slotted spoons, remove the ham from the stock and put it aside until it's cool enough to handle. Pick the meat into small bite-sized pieces, discarding any bone, sinew or cartilage. Pass the stock through a fine sieve into a bowl.

Wash the clams well to remove any sand and leave them to drain. Pod the peas.

Place a deep pot with a lid over a high heat. Tip the clams into the pot with 800ml of the ham hock stock. Put the lid back on and cook for 1 to 2 minutes until all the clams have opened. Add in the butter and the peas and cook for a minute more.

Mix the pieces of ham through and serve in bowls.

Mackerel with basil and smoked almond sauce

The best fish in the sea. If there's ever the opportunity to cook with mackerel, I'll always take it – it has an incredible flavour and is so versatile.

SERVES 4

ROASTED TOMATOES
12 cherry tomatoes, halved
sugar
salt
olive oil

SMOKED ALMOND SAUCE
60g spinach
40g smoked almonds, plus a few for garnish
50g basil
200ml almond milk
2 tbsp sunflower oil
juice of ¼ lemon
salt

2 whole mackerel, gutted and filleted (page 16)
fine salt
sunflower oil

Preheat your oven to 70°c fan.

Place the tomatoes on a greaseproof paper-lined tray. Sprinkle with a decent pinch of sugar and salt and drizzle with olive oil. Cook in the oven for an hour, checking them after 30 minutes, by which time they should be slightly softened.

Bring a pot of salted water to the boil and add the spinach. Blanch for 30 seconds, then put it into iced water. Drain and squeeze out the excess water and put into a blender. Add the smoked almonds, basil, almond milk, sunflower oil, lemon juice and a pinch of salt. Blitz until smooth, then taste and add more salt if needed. Pass the sauce through a sieve into a jug.

Roughly chop the smoked almonds reserved for the garnish and set aside.

Season the mackerel fillets all over with a little fine salt. Place a frying pan over a medium heat and add a little oil. Put the mackerel fillets in, skin-side down: they might curl up slightly as they cook so apply a little pressure to keep them flat and help get the skin crispy. After 2 minutes, turn the fish and cook for a minute on the other side.

Place a fillet on each plate, then add the roasted tomatoes and drizzle the sauce around them. Sprinkle over the chopped smoked almonds.

Hake with green goddess

I discovered green goddess sauce during lockdown when we were making hot barbecue food to take away. It's very worthy of its name and brightens any dish. Sharp, salty, creamy, fresh and so, so moreish.

SERVES 4

400g clams
250ml pickle liquor (page 280)
200g fregola
350g butternut squash, peeled, deseeded and cut into 1cm dice
1 tsp sunflower oil
4 hake fillets weighing about 140g each, with skin on
30g pumpkin seeds, toasted (page 23)
salt

GREEN GODDESS
120ml sour cream
120ml mayonnaise (page 280) or Hellmann's
60ml lemon juice
50g basil
3 spring onions, roughly chopped
1 garlic clove, thinly sliced
1 tsp sea salt

Preheat your oven to 175°c fan.

Run the clams under cold water to rinse off any sand. Put about 5cm of water into a pot with a lid and bring to a boil. Put the clams into the pot and replace the lid, then cook for 1 to 2 minutes until the shells have opened. Strain through a sieve and discard any clams that haven't opened, then set the rest aside until they are cool enough to handle. Remove the clam meat from the shells and cover with the pickle liquor.

To make the green goddess dressing, simply place the sour cream, mayo, lemon juice, basil, spring onions, garlic and salt in a blender and blitz until smooth.

Taste and adjust the seasoning if necessary: you want it to be quite zingy and fresh, so add more lemon juice if you think it needs it. Keep at room temperature.

Cook the fregola in a pot of boiling, salty water for 6 to 8 minutes until it's tender, then strain it and set aside.

Over a medium-high heat, sauté the butternut squash in a pan with the sunflower oil and a pinch of salt until just cooked, which should take 5 minutes.

Season the hake fillets on both sides and place them on an oiled piece of greaseproof paper on a baking tray. Cook in the oven until just cooked through – 8 minutes for fillets 4 to 5cm thick, 6 minutes if they're thinner.

While the fish is cooking, put the cooked fregola in a pot with a third of the green goddess and warm it over a medium heat. When it's hot, take it off the heat and stir through the rest of the green goddess. Add the butternut squash, pumpkin seeds and drained pickled clams and mix through.

Spoon the fregola into your serving dishes and scatter over the toasted pumpkin seeds. Carefully remove the skin from the hake fillets, then place on top of the fregola.

Roasted lamb rack with labneh and sweetheart cabbage

Ask your butcher to French trim the racks, just for that extra bit of wow factor.

SERVES 4

LABNEH
finely grated zest of 1 lemon
½ tsp sea salt
200g Greek yoghurt

LAMB RACK
1 tsp ground cumin
1 tsp garlic powder
1 tsp onion powder
1 tsp sea salt
1 tbsp sunflower oil
2 lamb racks weighing approx. 1kg
50g butter
3 sprigs of thyme

400g Chantenay carrots, peeled and trimmed
100g butter
1 sweetheart cabbage, halved
1 tsp sunflower oil
100g sugar snap peas, cut in half
1 tsp caraway seeds
salt

Start on the labneh as it needs to hang. Stir the lemon zest and the sea salt into the yoghurt and mix well. Line a sieve with a muslin cloth, then pour in the yoghurt and tie the ends of the cloth together. Hang for 1½ to 2 hours over a bowl; the longer you leave it, the firmer it'll get.

Make the lamb marinade: mix the ground cumin, garlic and onion powders, sea salt and sunflower oil together, and spread it liberally over the lamb racks. Leave to marinate for at least 30 minutes.

Preheat your oven to 180°c fan. Add a little oil to a pan and put it over a medium-high heat. Sear the lamb racks on all sides so they get a really good colour – about 7 or 8 minutes in total – then turn the heat down a little and add the butter and thyme. Allow the butter to melt and foam and use it to baste the racks a few times. Transfer to an ovenproof dish and place in the oven for 15 to 20 minutes, until the lamb has a temperature of 54°c. Remove from the oven and allow to rest for 10 minutes.

Put the carrots in a single layer in a wide, deep pan with 300ml water, 50g of the butter and a big pinch of salt. Cover loosely with a circle of tin foil and bring to a boil, then cook on a medium heat until the liquid has reduced. Don't shoogle the pan, just leave it to cook.

Blanch the halved cabbage in simmering salted water for 30 seconds. Drain, then cut each half into three wedges. Sear the cabbage in a hot pan with the sunflower oil until golden brown and caramelised all over, then add the remaining 50g butter and let it foam and melt. Put the cabbage into a warm serving dish. Add the sugar snaps to the pan, season and sauté until they're cooked. Mix them with the carrots and put into another serving dish. Toast the caraway seeds in a dry pan and scatter them on top.

Carve the lamb and serve with the vegetables and labneh alongside.

Lanark Blue and nectarine tarte tatin

One thing that we've always done at The Little Chartroom is a cheese dessert rather than a cheese selection. It's always fun to think up more elaborate dishes and combinations, like a cheese custard and gooseberry Paris-Brest, or toasted crumpets and whipped blue. One of my all-time favourites was this nectarine tarte tatin.

You'll need a 20cm-diameter frying pan that can go in the oven.

SERVES 4

PASTRY
250g plain flour
1 tsp salt
125g butter, diced
1 tbsp milk
1 egg, separated

400g caster sugar
4 nectarines, halved and stoned
20g demerara sugar
250g Lanark Blue
1 sprig of thyme, leaves picked (optional)

20cm ovenproof frying pan

To make the pastry, mix the flour and salt together in a bowl. Dice the butter into small pieces and rub through the flour until it's all incorporated and resembles breadcrumbs. (You can also do this in a food processor or stand mixer, for speed.) In a jug, mix the milk and egg yolk together and add 80ml water. Mix this into the butter and flour until it just starts to form a dough, then lightly knead it together with your hands. Shape the pastry into a fat disc about 4cm thick, wrap in cling film and place in the fridge to rest for at least 1 hour.

Preheat the oven to 180°c fan.

Place the caster sugar in a heavy-bottomed pot and place on a low heat. Allow the sugar to start melting and colouring – you can tip or shake the pot to move the sugar around so it melts evenly but try not to stir it as it might crystallise. Take it to an amber caramel and pour into your ovenproof frying pan. (You could make the caramel straight in the frying pan, but it is harder to control the temperature and stop it burning so I tend to do it in a separate pan.) Place the nectarine halves cut-side down on top of the caramel.

On a lightly floured surface, roll the pastry out to about 5mm thick. Cut out a 20cm circle and lay it on top of the nectarines, then tuck the pastry down around the edge of the pan. Brush with the egg white and evenly sprinkle over the demerara sugar. Bake the tarte tatin in the oven for 20 minutes, until the pastry is golden brown.

Allow it to cool slightly, then invert your serving plate over the pan and very carefully flip it all over, so the tarte tatin is turned out on the plate. Crumble over the Lanark Blue and scatter picked thyme leaves on top if you're using them.

Summer berries

This is a real celebration of berries. It's a simple dessert to make and put together, but the strawberry consommé and roasted vanilla cream both need a couple of hours to make and chill, so allow yourself some time.

SERVES 4

STRAWBERRY CONSOMMÉ
1kg frozen strawberries
50g sugar

SUMMER BERRIES
200g strawberries
200g blueberries
200g raspberries
200g blackberries
2 tbsp strawberry vinegar (page 276) or white balsamic vinegar
15g flaked almonds, toasted (page 23)

TO SERVE
1 recipe roasted vanilla cream (page 81)

Start with the strawberry consommé. Mix the frozen strawberries and the sugar in a heatproof bowl and cover with cling film. Put them over a pot of simmering water and cook very gently for an hour – you will see all the natural juices coming out of the fruit. Strain through a fine sieve or muslin and leave to drip through so you get every last bit of juice. You should get about 200ml. Don't squash the fruit down or you won't get a clear consommé. Allow to cool, then chill in the fridge. Next, make the roasted vanilla cream on page 81.

Cut the strawberries into 2cm pieces. Halve the blueberries and the raspberries and cut the blackberries in halves or thirds depending on how big they are. Put all the berries in your serving bowl and add the chilled strawberry consommé and the vinegar. Gently mix through, then scatter over the toasted flaked almonds. Serve with the roasted vanilla cream on the side for people to help themselves.

Chilled rice pudding

My childhood in a bowl… such a nostalgic dish for me. Rice pudding works with every flavour, but the fresh apricots with the crunchy ginger biscuits in this one are epic.

SERVES 4

RICE PUDDING
50g butter
110g pudding or arborio rice
400ml milk
500ml double cream
80g sugar
seeds from 1 vanilla pod
salt

GINGER BISCUITS
50g butter
50g golden syrup
20g treacle
20g light brown soft sugar
60g self-raising flour
25g small rolled oats
½ tsp ground ginger
1 tbsp beaten egg
1 tbsp milk
20g stem ginger, finely chopped

TO SERVE
4 fresh apricots, stoned and cut into pieces
10g bee pollen
10g edible flowers

Make the rice pudding first. Melt the butter in a heavy bottomed pan, then stir in the rice and cook for a few minutes so the rice toasts a little. Stir in the milk, cream, sugar and vanilla seeds and gently cook on a medium heat for 20 to 35 minutes, stirring frequently so it doesn't catch and burn, until the rice is tender. How long it takes will vary depending on the age of your rice so keep checking and cooking until it is done. Add a pinch of salt at the end to balance the sweetness. Strain the rice pudding through a sieve and put the pudding in one bowl and the cooking liquid in another. Chill both in the fridge for at least 45 minutes.

While the rice pudding is chilling, make your ginger biscuits. Preheat your oven to 180°c fan and line a baking tray with some greaseproof paper.

In a small pot, melt the butter with the golden syrup, treacle and light brown sugar and warm until the sugar has dissolved. In a bowl, mix the flour, oats and ground ginger together. Stir this into the sugar mixture in the pan, then add the beaten egg, milk and finely chopped stem ginger and mix until incorporated. Put spoonfuls of the batter on your greaseproof-lined tray and bake for 15 to 20 minutes, until golden and crisp. Leave the biscuits to cool on a wire rack and then roughly chop.

When you're ready to serve, gradually add the chilled cooking liquid back into the rice to get the consistency you like. Put the rice pudding in a serving bowl and top with the broken-up ginger biscuits, apricot pieces, bee pollen and edible flowers.

Lemon thyme parfait with grilled peaches

Fragrant lemon thyme and smoky sweet peaches – delicious! Serve it quite quickly as the parfait will start to melt when the warm fruit goes on.

SERVES 6

LEMON THYME PARFAIT

300ml whipping cream
20g lemon thyme
10 egg yolks
250g sugar

TO FINISH

4 peaches
50g flaked almonds, toasted (page 23)
5g lemon thyme, leaves picked

24 × 10 × 7cm loaf tin

First, lightly grease your loaf tin, then line it with greaseproof paper, allowing a little overhang to help get the finished parfait out once frozen.

Gently heat the cream until it is steaming, but don't allow it to boil. Add the sprigs of lemon thyme and leave to infuse for 30 minutes to an hour. Strain the cream through a sieve and put it into the fridge until it is completely cold.

In a stand mixer or a large bowl, whisk the egg yolks until pale.

In a pot, bring 180ml water to the boil and add the sugar. Bring it back to the boil and cook until the sugar has dissolved and the syrup reaches 120°c on a sugar thermometer.

Remove from the heat and slowly and carefully pour the syrup into the egg yolks with the mixer running. Whisk continuously on a high speed for 3 to 4 minutes until the mix has firmed up. Leave to cool for 10 minutes.

Whisk the thyme-infused cream to soft peaks, then fold it through the cooled egg mixture.

Pour into the lined loaf tin and put into the freezer for at least 24 hours, until fully frozen.

Halve the peaches and discard the stones. Cut each half into four wedges and grill on a barbecue or griddle (or under the grill in your oven), just until the peaches get some colour and start to soften.

Turn the parfait upside down on your serving plate, and using the paper gently ease it out of the tin. Scatter the peaches, almonds and thyme over the top of the parfait and serve in thick slices.

Summer pudding

A traditional summer pudding is stuffed with mixed berries. Hamish (the head chef at Eleanore) came up with the wonderful idea of adding in a bavarois, lightening the whole dish with the silky, light custard. It's absolutely delicious.

SERVES 6–8

500g frozen mixed berries
100g caster sugar
100g blueberries
100g raspberries
100g strawberries
100g blackberries
100g currants (a mix of red and black, or whatever is available)
5 slices of medium-sliced soft, white bread
a few sprigs of lemon verbena, picked

BAVAROIS
50g caster sugar
½ tbsp cornflour
75ml buttermilk or crème fraîche
1 medium egg
juice of 1 lemon
180ml double cream
1 leaf platinum gelatine

glass mixing bowl about 15cm in diameter and 8cm in height

In a heatproof bowl, mix the frozen berries with the caster sugar and then cover with cling film. Put the bowl over a pot of gently simmering water and leave it to cook for about an hour, by which time a lot of juice will have come out of the fruit, creating a glorious berry consommé. Strain the berries through a sieve into a bowl to catch all the consommé – don't press the berries in the sieve or you will make it cloudy, just leave them sitting there for about 30 minutes to allow all the liquid to drip out.

Next, make the bavarois. In a heatproof bowl, whisk together the sugar, cornflour, buttermilk, egg, lemon juice and 125ml of the double cream. Place the bowl over a pan of simmering water and take it to 80°C, stirring continuously, until the custard has thickened and coats the back of a spoon. Remove from the heat.

Bloom the gelatine in cold water for 5 minutes, then squeeze out the excess water and add the softened leaf to the custard, mixing thoroughly until it has dissolved. Leave the bavarois to cool – you can speed this up by putting the bowl over ice, with a sheet of cling film pressed on to the surface of the custard to stop it from forming a skin. Once it is completely cool, lightly whip the remaining 55ml double cream to soft peaks, then fold it through the custard.

You want all the fruit for the filling to be in similar-sized pieces, so cut the blueberries and raspberries in half, quarter the strawberries and cut the blackberries into thirds if they're big. Leave the currants as they are. Fold half of the berries through the bavarois, leaving the rest to decorate your pudding.

Recipe continues overleaf

Now to build your summer pudding. Line your bowl with cling film, leaving plenty overhanging the rim. Set a wire rack over a baking tray. Now, remove the crusts from the bread and cut two of the slices in half lengthways to give you four rectangles. Cut two other slices on the diagonal so you have four triangles. Dip the rectangles of bread into the berry consommé for about 20 seconds each side, then place on to the wire rack to drain for a few minutes. Imagine your bowl is like a clock face: place a soaked rectangle of bread at 12 and another at 6 so they meet in the middle. Place the other rectangles at 3 and 9 so they all join neatly at the base of the bowl, with no gaps. Take one of the unsoaked triangles and trim it so it fits perfectly in the gap between two of the rectangles. Use this piece as a template to trim the remaining triangles, then dip them all in the consommé for 20 seconds per side and put on the wire rack to drain. Fit the soaked triangles in between the rectangles so the bowl is completely lined with soaked bread, then pile in your bavarois mix. Soak and drain the final piece of bread, then place it on top of the bavarois and fold in the edges of bread poking up around the sides. Fold over the overhanging cling film, then place your pudding in the fridge to set for at least 2 hours.

Once set, unfold the cling film and invert a serving plate on top of the bowl. Flip everything over so the pudding is on your serving plate, then remove the bowl and peel away the cling film. Arrange the reserved berries around the pudding and garnish with a few leaves of lemon verbena.

Cherry, pistachio and marzipan trifle

This dessert is a real crowd pleaser. Good, boozy cherries are the key! You need to infuse the cherries for a minimum of 48 hours (and a maximum of a week). If you don't have time, then buy three 370g jars of cherries in kirsch and use the liquid to make your cherry jelly.

Between adding each layer, wipe the inside of your trifle dish free of any smears so you get a lovely clean finish.

SERVES 8, GENEROUSLY

BOOZY CHERRY JELLY

125g caster sugar
425ml cherry brandy
600g fresh cherries, stems and stones discarded
5 platinum gelatine leaves

PISTACHIO CAKE

3 eggs
150g caster sugar
100g butter, melted
50ml sunflower oil
150g pistachio flour
150g plain flour
¼ tsp salt

MARZIPAN CUSTARD

500ml milk
180g marzipan, grated
1 platinum gelatine leaves
7 egg yolks
40g custard powder

400ml double cream
100g pistachios, toasted (page 23) and roughly chopped

20cm cake tin, lined
20cm glass trifle dish, preferably flat bottomed

At least 48 hours before you want to eat the trifle, start on the cherries. Put the sugar in a pot with 125ml water and bring to a simmer, stirring to make sure the sugar has all dissolved. Take off the heat and add the cherry brandy. Put your stoned cherries into a container or jar with a lid, then pour over the cherry booze. Put the lid on and leave to infuse.

On the day you are going to serve the trifle, start by making the pistachio cake. Preheat your oven to 170°C fan.

Beat the eggs and sugar together in a large bowl, then mix in the melted butter and oil.

In another bowl, mix the pistachio flour, plain flour and salt together. Fold the dry ingredients through the egg/sugar mix until well combined, then pour the batter into your lined cake tin. Bake for 30 minutes, until a skewer inserted into the middle comes out clean. Turn it out of the tin and leave to cool on a wire rack. Once the sponge is cool, trim off the crust of the cake so all the golden bits are removed and the beautiful green sponge is on show. Weigh out 425g and break it up with your hands, then lightly press into the base of your trifle dish. Put it into the fridge for an hour.

Strain the booze-infused cherries over a pot to catch the liquid, and scatter them over the pistachio sponge in your trifle dish. Warm the cherry liquid over a low heat. Bloom the gelatine in a bowl of cold water for 5 minutes, then squeeze out any excess liquid and add the gelatine to the warm cherry juice. Stir until it has all completely dissolved, then put the jelly aside to cool. When it's just starting to set, pour half of the jelly into the trifle dish so it soaks into the sponge and put it back into the fridge. Keep the remaining jelly at room temperature. Once the jelly in the trifle bowl has set, pour the other half on top and put back in the fridge to set – if the jelly has set too much to pour, you might need to reheat it slightly.

Recipe continues overleaf

Finally, make the marzipan custard. Put the milk in a pot over a medium heat and whisk in the grated marzipan. Heat until the milk is steaming and the marzipan has melted. Bloom the gelatine in a bowl of cold water for 5 minutes. In a bowl, whisk the egg yolks and custard powder together. Whisk a small amount of the hot milk mix into the yolks, then add the rest of it in a thin stream, whisking continuously. Return all the mix to the pan and cook over a low heat, stirring all the time, until it reaches 82°c and has thickened enough that you can draw a line in it on the back of a spoon. Squeeze out any excess water from the gelatine leaves, then add them to the custard and stir until completely dissolved. Pour into a bowl and press a piece of cling film on to the surface to stop a skin forming. Put the custard over ice or in the fridge to cool.

Once the custard is completely cool, blitz it thoroughly in a blender, then carefully spread it on top of the cherry jelly in a thick layer. Return the trifle to the fridge.

Whip the cream, spread it on top of the custard and sprinkle with chopped, toasted pistachios.

Summer dinner party menu

I'm a feeder, regardless of the time of year. If you come to my house for dinner, you won't leave hungry! What I love about a dinner party is the grazing that inevitably happens when everyone is relaxed, chatting, eating and drinking. These dishes are perfect for this.

Meaty koftas in the middle of the table balanced with a clean, fresh salad.

Whole cooked turbot with the most delicious braised squid and ratatouille.

And a silky custard tart with sweet raspberries to round off proceedings!

Strawberry and ginger hi-ball

Summer in a glass: long, refreshing and not too boozy.

SERVES 1

35ml dark rum
25ml strawberry syrup
200ml ginger beer

Mix the dark rum and strawberry syrup together in a tall glass over ice, then top up with ginger beer.

Strawberry syrup

This will make more than you need to make a cocktail, but it can be kept for up to a week in the fridge and is delicious with lemonade or soda.

MAKES 300ML

300g strawberries
200g sugar
300ml water

Cut the stems off the strawberries, then cut them in half. Put them in a pan with the sugar and 300ml water and bring to a simmer over a medium heat. Simmer gently for 10 minutes, until syrupy. Leave to cool a little and then strain into a bottle or Kilner jar.

Pork kofta with apple molasses

You need a bit of fat to make these kofta properly juicy, so if you're unable to get pork fat, a fatty piece of pork belly will work well too. The apple juice takes time to get to the right consistency, but it's worth it to get lovely, sweet, sticky molasses.

SERVES 6

APPLE MOLASSES
1l apple juice
50ml cider vinegar
50g treacle

PORK KOFTA
sunflower oil
2 onions, finely diced
500g pork mince
200g minced pork fat
    (or fatty pork belly)
½ tsp ground cumin
½ tsp cracked black pepper
½ tsp garlic powder
½ tsp mustard powder
1 tbsp salt
20g white sesame seeds

CRISPY GREEN VEG
sunflower oil
100g sugar snaps, thinly sliced
½ hispi or sweetheart cabbage,
    cored and thinly sliced
2 spring onions, thinly sliced
1 Granny Smith apple, grated
40g peanuts, toasted and cut in halves
1 tbsp cold-pressed rapeseed oil

8 metal skewers

To make the apple molasses, pour the apple juice into a large, heavy-bottomed pot and add the apple vinegar and treacle. Boil over a medium-high heat for 45 minutes to an hour, until it has reduced down to about 150 to 200ml and has a syrupy consistency. Turn the heat down a little as it reduces, and watch it closely as you get to the end of the cooking time so it doesn't burn.

To make the koftas, add enough sunflower oil to cover the base of your pan and put over a medium heat, then add the diced onions and a pinch of salt. Sauté until they are soft and translucent. Put the pork mince and fat into a large bowl and add the cooked onion, cumin, cracked black pepper, garlic and mustard powders and salt. Mix everything together with your hands, then divide into eight and mould each piece around a metal skewer. Put in the fridge for at least 30 minutes to firm up.

Preheat your oven to 175°c fan. Using a griddle or barbecue, sear the koftas for 2 minutes on each side until they have a nice char on them, then put them in the oven for 5 minutes. Take out and brush all over with the apple molasses, then return to the oven for 2 minutes. Once they're out of the oven, brush them with more molasses and sprinkle with sesame seeds.

In a hot pan with a little oil, flash fry the thinly sliced sugar snaps, hispi and spring onion for no longer than 30 seconds. Stir through the grated apple and toasted peanuts.

Mix 2 tablespoons of the apple molasses with the cold-pressed rapeseed oil and dress the crispy veg with it.

Whole baked turbot with braised squid ratatouille

If possible, ask your fishmonger to clean your squid, but if that's not an option it's easy to do.

SERVES 6

BRAISED SQUID RATATOUILLE
1kg whole squid, cleaned
sunflower oil
4 banana shallots, diced
4 garlic cloves, grated
8 tbsp tomato purée
150ml white wine
500ml chicken stock (page 278)
4 plum tomatoes
1 small yellow courgette
1 small green courgette
3 baby aubergines
salt

1 turbot, weighing about 3kg
1 tbsp sunflower oil
1 tbsp sea salt

Preheat your oven to 160°c fan.

Begin with the squid. If they haven't been cleaned already, remove the head and tentacles from the body – they can be pulled out with your hand. Cut the tentacles just below the eyes and remove the hard beak from the centre, then wash the tentacles in cold water. Discard the eyes and innards.

Next, check inside the body for the quill (which is long and feels like plastic). This can be pulled out and discarded. Pull the wings off the side of the body and thoroughly wash the squid inside and out with cold water, removing any bits that are left.

Cut the squid body down one side so it opens and lies flat on your board. Cut in half and slice as thinly as you can, around 2mm. Thinly slice the tentacles as well.

Put a little oil into a casserole pot with a lid and put it over a high heat. Carefully tip all the sliced squid and the tentacles into the pot, then cover and leave to cook for 2 minutes. Drain in a colander.

In the same pot over a medium heat, add a little more oil and sauté the diced shallots and grated garlic until soft. Add in the tomato purée and a pinch of sea salt and cook for 2 minutes, stirring so it doesn't stick. Return the squid to the pan and deglaze with the white wine. Reduce until almost dry, then pour in the chicken stock. If you're using shop-bought chicken stock, make sure it doesn't taste too salty; if it does, add about 100ml water. Pop the lid back on the casserole and place in the oven for about an hour, by which time the squid should be soft and tender and the liquid should have reduced and be coating the squid. (Cook for a little longer if you think it needs it.) Set the squid aside and increase the oven temperature to 175°c fan.

Blanch the plum tomatoes for 30 seconds in boiling water, then peel off the skins. Very thinly slice the yellow and green courgettes, the aubergines and the tomatoes to 2.5mm thick and sprinkle with a little fine salt.

Transfer the braised squid to an ovenproof serving dish. Working from the outside in, arrange the sliced vegetables in a spiral on top of the squid. We make the central rosette on a chopping board, then pick it up on the flat of a knife and lay it in the middle for a really neat finish. Cut out a circle of greaseproof paper and put it on top of the ratatouille, then put the casserole back in the oven to bake for 20 minutes.

Place the turbot on a large tray and drizzle over the oil and sprinkle with sea salt. Bake in the oven for 25 minutes. You can check it is cooked by poking a skewer into the thickest part of the flesh: if it meets any resistance, the fish needs a little longer.

Serve alongside the braised squid ratatouille.

Raspberry custard tart

Fill your baked tart case while it's on the shelf in the oven – this helps prevent stress, spillages and possible disasters!

SERVES 6

1 recipe sweet pastry, rested (page 282)
1 egg, beaten

FILLING
5 eggs
180g sugar
2 tbsp plain flour
400ml buttermilk
200ml double cream
2 lemons
salt
450g raspberries
2 tsp raspberry vinegar or white balsamic
60g pistachios, toasted and roughly chopped
a square of white chocolate (for grating)

25cm tart tin

Preheat your oven to 180°c fan.

On a well-floured worktop, roll your pastry into a circle about 30cm in diameter and 5mm thick – it needs to be a large enough piece to fit into your tart case with excess pastry hanging over the edge. Keep moving the pastry, making sure it doesn't stick to the worktop. Wrap the pastry around your rolling pin to transfer it to the tart case, then carefully work the pastry into the base of the tart case, leaving the excess hanging over the edge. Cover the pastry with two sheets of cling film and fill with ceramic cooking beans – I prefer to use ceramic beans as they retain the heat and cook the pastry more evenly. Rest in the fridge for 30 minutes.

Put the pastry case in the oven and bake for 20 minutes. Then carefully pull one side of the cling film up and check that the pastry is fully cooked. If it's still a little raw, return to the oven for a few more minutes with the cling film and beans still in place. Once it's cooked, carefully remove the beans and cling film and put the pastry case back in the oven for 5 minutes until it is golden brown.

Brush the base and sides of the pastry with a thin layer of beaten egg and pop back in the oven for a minute. This helps create a seal so the custard won't seep through any small holes. (It won't work if the holes are big though, so make sure they're patched up from the start.)

Set aside to cool in the tin, then use a vegetable peeler to gently shave off the excess pastry around the edges of the tart.

Reduce your oven temp to 120°c fan. In a bowl, whisk the eggs, sugar and flour together, then add the buttermilk and cream. Zest one of the lemons into the mix, then juice both of them and add that along with a pinch of salt. Whisk until fully combined and then transfer to a big jug.

Place the tart case on a baking tray in the oven and then pull the oven shelf halfway out. Carefully and slowly pour the custard into the case – it will be quite full – then gently push the oven shelf back in and close the door. After 40 minutes check the tart: you want it to be mostly firm with a slight wobble in the middle. Cook for another 5 minutes if necessary, checking regularly. Allow the tart to cool completely and then carefully remove it from the tin and put it on a large flat plate.

Cut the raspberries in half and arrange on the top of the tart, some with the cut side facing up. Drizzle over the vinegar and finish with the chopped pistachios and finely grated white chocolate.

Autumn

As the nights start to draw in and the leaves change from green to brown, game, wild mushrooms, plums and pumpkins are what come to mind. Greengages and damsons are my favourite, and it's always a race to get them in their short window – blink and they're gone!

Oysters with blackberry and apple

Sweet, sharp, striking. A well-dressed oyster is a great way to start any meal and it will never fail to impress your guests.

SERVES 4

1 Pink Lady apple
8 oysters, shucked (page 10)
8 tsp blackberry vinegar (page 276)
cold-pressed rapeseed oil

Peel and cut the core out of the apple, then cut into small dice. Spoon a teaspoon of apple dice on top of each oyster, followed by a teaspoon of blackberry vinegar. Add 3 drops of rapeseed oil onto each oyster.

That's it. Enjoy!

Mallard rillettes on duck fat toast

Rillettes are so good to snack on. If you can, allow time to salt the mallard legs – it's not a necessity but it improves the flavour.

I love to use mallard – it has a wonderful flavour, with subtle gamey notes that work well with many ingredients. You'll need to buy four whole mallard for this recipe, but you can either roast the rest of the bird or cut off the breasts and use them instead of duck breasts in the smoked duck salad recipe on page 218. And, of course, you could use two duck legs instead and cook them in exactly the same way.

SERVES 4 OR 8 AS A SNACK

MALLARD RILLETTES
8 mallard legs (about 400g total)
100g coarse salt
600g duck fat
4 garlic cloves, unpeeled and halved
10g thyme
4 bay leaves
4 spring onions, thinly sliced
100g cornichons, quartered lengthways and finely chopped
10g chives, finely chopped
sea salt

TO SERVE
sunflower oil
400g raw red beetroot, peeled and grated
1 Pink Lady apple, grated
50g demerara sugar
40g cider vinegar
1 tsp salt
4 slices of sourdough bread

Put the mallard legs in a dish and cover with the coarse salt. Leave them for an hour, then wash the salt off and pat the legs dry.

Melt the duck fat in a pot over low heat, then add the mallard legs, garlic, thyme and bay leaves, making sure the legs are completely submerged. Bring to a simmer, then turn the heat down and leave it to tick over for 1 to 1½ hours, until the meat is tender and falling off the bone.

Once they're cooked, take the legs out of the fat and leave to cool, then pick the meat, discarding the bones, skin and any cartilage. Put the meat in a bowl and, with two forks or your hands, work it until it's completely shredded with no solid bits.

Add the sliced spring onions, cornichons and finely chopped chives and mix thoroughly, adding about 4 tablespoons of duck fat to bind everything together. Have a taste and add a pinch of salt if it's needed, then pop the rillettes into a container and place in the fridge to set.

Put enough oil in a pot to cover the base, and add the grated beetroot. Sweat over a medium heat for about 5 minutes until it is almost cooked, then stir in the grated apple, sugar, vinegar and salt and continue cooking until all the liquid has reduced. Leave to cool.

Toast the bread and brush with a little of the duck fat. Cut each slice in half and spoon a pile of the mallard rillettes on to each one, then top with a spoonful of beetroot.

Confit duck milk buns

We made these buns to accompany a duck parfait starter in the restaurant and they were delicious just by themselves. This recipe isn't labour-intensive but some of the processes are quite long. The confit duck and ketchup can be made in advance, but the milk bun dough is at its best made on the day.

MAKES 10 BUNS

CONFIT DUCK LEG
2 duck legs
100g coarse salt
500g duck fat
1 orange
1 cinnamon stick
1 star anise
2 cloves
1 bunch of thyme
1 tsp allspice

MILK BUN DOUGH
160g strong flour
80ml whole milk
1½ tsp milk powder
25g sugar
½ tsp salt
½ sachet (3.5g) instant dried yeast
1 egg, beaten
40g softened butter
1 egg yolk for glazing
flaky sea salt

Put the duck legs in a flat container and cover them with the coarse salt, then pop them in the fridge for 1 hour. Wash the salt off and pat the meat dry with some paper towels.

Melt the duck fat in a pot and then put in the duck legs, making sure they are fully submerged. Use a veg peeler to peel long strips of orange zest off the orange, and add them to the pot along with the cinnamon stick, star anise, cloves and thyme (keeping the rest of the orange, as you'll need the juice later). Bring it up to a very slow simmer and gently cook for 2 to 3 hours until the meat is falling off the bone.

While the duck is cooking, start on your milk bun dough. In a small pot, mix 10g of the flour and 20ml of the milk with 20ml water and cook, stirring continuously, over a medium-low heat until it thickens to a stiff paste. Allow to cool. This is your starter dough.

In a stand mixer with the dough hook fitted, mix the remaining 150g flour with the milk powder, sugar, salt and yeast. Add the rest of the milk (60ml), the egg and the starter dough and mix until fully incorporated, then add in the softened butter and mix on a low speed for 5 minutes (or knead it by hand if you're not using a mixer). Transfer the dough to an oiled bowl and cover with cling film. Leave to prove at room temperature for 2 hours, until the dough has doubled in size.

Once the duck legs are cooked, take them out of the fat and leave to cool, then pick off the meat, discarding the bones, skin and any cartilage. Roughly chop the meat, and mix through the allspice, the juice of half of the orange you peeled earlier and 2 tablespoons of duck fat. Divide into ten equal-sized portions and roll them into balls. Pop them into the fridge on a greaseproof-lined tray to firm up.

Once your milk dough has proved, knock it back and portion into ten 30g pieces. It's quite a soft dough, so use a touch of oil on the palm of your hands and roll each piece into a ball, then put them on a deep tray lined with greaseproof paper. Cover with cling film and put in the fridge for 20 to 30 minutes.

Now, take a ball of dough and slightly flatten it, then wrap it around a ball of the confit duck filling, pinching it together so the meat is completely encased. Try not to stretch the dough too much. Using the worktop and the palm of your hand, mould it into a smooth ball – again, use a touch of oil on your hands if the dough is sticking. Repeat with the remaining dough and confit duck balls.

Transfer the buns to a deep, greaseproof-lined tray, and cover with cling film. Leave to prove at room temperature for 1 to 2 hours, until they've doubled in size.

Preheat the oven to 175°c fan. Brush each bun generously with egg yolk, making sure to brush the sides too, and sprinkle over some flaky sea salt. Bake the buns for 12 minutes, then let them cool a little on a wire rack. Serve warm with a generous dollop of plum ketchup.

Plum ketchup

MAKES 450ML

4 shallots, thinly sliced
1 tbsp oil
8 plums, stoned and quartered
50g dark brown soft sugar
50ml red wine vinegar
50g treacle

In a pot, sweat down the shallots in the oil until they start to soften, then add in the plums, dark brown soft sugar, red wine vinegar and treacle. Cook over a low heat until the plums are very soft and only a little liquid is left, about 30 minutes. Blend to a smooth purée.

Pumpkin and fresh cheese tarts

Texture is so important in a dish, and this has bags of it! Pumpkin and fresh cheese on a base of courgette marmalade make a delicious combo, and the extra crunch of toasted pumpkin seeds really elevates these little tarts.

SERVES 4

COURGETTE MARMALADE
250g courgette, cut into 1cm dice
1 tbsp oil
3 tbsp white wine vinegar
2 tbsp caster sugar
fine salt

½ recipe cream cheese pastry (page 281)
400g pumpkin or butternut squash, peeled and deseeded
1 tbsp sunflower oil
2 tbsp maple syrup
2 tsp good-quality olive oil
1 tbsp pickle liquor (page 280) or cider/white wine vinegar
1 recipe fresh cheese (page 280), crumbled
20g pumpkin seeds, toasted
micro herbs
salt

four 9cm fluted tart cases

To make the courgette marmalade, put the courgette dice in a pot with the oil and sweat down over a medium heat for 10 minutes. Add the vinegar, sugar and a pinch of salt and continue cooking until all the liquid has evaporated. Set aside to cool.

Cut the cream cheese pastry into four equal pieces and roll to 5mm thick on a lightly floured worktop. Push a piece of pastry into each of your tart tins, making sure it is well pressed in, then trim off any excess. Cut four pieces of cling film and place one inside each tart, allowing enough to overhang the edges. Fill with ceramic baking beans then pop the tarts in the fridge to rest for 30 minutes.

Preheat the oven to 175°c fan. Put the tart cases on a baking tray and bake in the oven for 12 to 14 minutes until the pastry is crispy and golden brown. The shape and size of the tins will affect the cooking time so keep an eye on them. If the base still looks a little raw, remove the beans and cling film and pop the tarts back in the oven for another 2 or 3 minutes. Leave to cool on a wire rack.

Cut the pumpkin into bite-sized pieces about 5cm long and 1cm thick, then put a couple of pieces aside to do shavings for the garnish. Season with a pinch of fine salt, and gently pan fry the pumpkin on each side in the tablespoon of oil until tender and golden.

Whisk the maple syrup with the olive oil and add the pickle liquor if you have it (or cider or white wine vinegar with a small pinch of sea salt if you don't). Using a potato peeler, shave some ribbons from the reserved raw pumpkin, then drizzle them with a little dressing and leave to sit for a couple of minutes.

Place a spoon of courgette marmalade in the base of each tart, then build up with the pan-fried pumpkin, crumbled fresh cheese and pumpkin seeds. Garnish with some dressed pumpkin ribbons and drizzle generously with the maple dressing.

Finish with micro herbs.

Pigeon, chicory and blackberry tarts

Sweet berries, bitter chicory and smoky, juicy pigeon – the perfect combo.

SERVES 4

½ recipe cream cheese pastry (page 281)
sunflower oil
6 pigeon breasts, skin on if possible
1 tbsp blackberry vinegar (page 276)
2 tbsp good-quality olive oil
50g blackberries
50g walnuts, toasted (page 23)
a few mustard frills
sea salt

CHICORY MARMALADE
4 chicory heads
40g butter
60g caster sugar
fine salt

four 10cm tart tins with removeable bases

Cut the pastry into four equal pieces. On a lightly floured worktop, roll out each piece to about 5mm thick and place into your tart tins, making sure each piece is pressed into the edges. Trim off any excess, then put a piece of cling film on top of each one so it overlaps the edges. Fill with ceramic beans (they help the pastry cook more evenly than dried beans) and put in the fridge to rest for 30 minutes – this will stop the pastry from shrinking too much as it cooks.

Whilst the pastry is resting you can make the chicory marmalade. Trim the bottom of the chicory heads, then cut them into quarters. Trim off the core from each quarter then thinly slice them. Melt the butter in a pot over a medium-low heat, then add the sliced chicory and cook for 10 minutes, stirring frequently. Mix in the sugar and cook for another 10 minutes, until the liquid has become syrupy and coats the chicory. Add a good pinch of salt, taste and adjust the seasoning if you think it needs it.

Preheat your oven to 175°c fan. Bake the pastry cases in the oven for 12 to 14 minutes until the pastry is golden brown. Remove the cling film and beans, and if the base needs to be cooked a little more pop them back in the oven for 2 to 3 minutes, until golden.

Put a splash of oil into a frying pan over a medium-high heat. Season the pigeon breasts, then put them in the hot pan, skin-side down, and cook for 2 minutes. Flip them and cook for another 2 minutes on the other side, then remove from the pan and allow to rest for 5 minutes.

In a little bowl, mix the blackberry vinegar with the olive oil and add a pinch of salt. Cut the blackberries into smallish pieces and dress in the blackberry vinaigrette.

Remove the skin from the pigeon breasts and cut the meat into 1cm thick slices.

Now build the tarts: spread a thickish layer of chicory marmalade in the bottom of each pastry case and cover with slices of pigeon. Arrange the dressed blackberries and walnuts on top and garnish with a few leaves of mustard frill.

Carrot and goat's cheese salad

One of my favourite goat's cheeses is Blackmount, which is made by Selina Cairns, an amazing Scottish cheesemaker. It is punchy and tart, which works perfectly with all the carrot flavours.

SERVES 4

500g large carrots, peeled
150ml pickle liquor (page 280)
1 tbsp sunflower oil
200ml carrot juice
20–24 baby rainbow carrots
50g butter
100g goat's cheese
100g hazelnuts, toasted
   (page 23) and cut in half
red mustard frills
fine salt

Take the large carrots, then thinly slice one of them and put the slices into a bowl. Cut another two of them in half lengthways and set aside, then roughly chop the carrots you've got left. Warm the pickle liquor and pour it over the thinly sliced carrots.

In a pot heat the oil, then add the chopped carrot and season with some salt. Sauté over a medium heat for 5 to 10 minutes, then pour over the carrot juice. Bring to a simmer and cook until the carrots are tender and the pan is almost dry, then blend to a smooth purée. Taste and adjust the seasoning.

Wash and trim the baby rainbow carrots, leaving a little bit of the leaf stem at the top, then peel them. Put the carrots in a frying pan with a pinch of salt, 200ml water and 25g of the butter, then place a loose tin foil 'lid' on top so the water can evaporate. Cook on a high heat but keep an eye on it – you want all the water to evaporate but you don't want the carrots to burn. This is a great technique to keep all the flavour in the carrot. Put them into a dish to cool.

In the same frying pan, cook the reserved carrot halves in the same way with the remaining butter and 200ml water. You need to cook them separately as they'll take longer than the baby carrots.

To serve, place a few dollops of purée on each plate, then randomly arrange the carrot halves, baby rainbow carrots and pickled carrots on top. Finish by crumbling over the goat's cheese and then sprinkle with some toasted hazelnuts and a few red mustard frills.

Cured sea trout with apple

This is a classic combo that I go back to time and time again. The curing for the trout can be done overnight – it takes 8 hours – and then it needs to dry for a couple of hours. Ask your fishmonger to skin and pin-bone the trout for you if possible.

SERVES 4

75g fine salt
75g caster sugar
300g sea trout fillet
3 Granny Smith apples
2 Braeburn apples
1 cucumber
2 tbsp white soy
1 tsp cider vinegar
4 tsp cold-pressed rapeseed oil
30g toasted flaked almonds (page 23)
60g smoked almonds, roughly chopped
1 tsp lemon juice

Mix the fine salt and sugar together.

Trim, skin and pin-bone the sea trout if it hasn't been done, then generously sprinkle it on each side with the fine salt and sugar mix. Leave for 8 hours, then rinse the cure off with cold water and put the fish on a metal rack in the fridge for a couple of hours to dry out.

Peel two of the Granny Smith apples and one of the Braeburns. Juice them with half of the cucumber (skin, seeds and all). Pour the juice into a blender with the white soy, cider vinegar, rapeseed oil and flaked almonds and blitz until smooth. Pass the dressing through a sieve into a jug and set aside.

Slice the cured sea trout into 5mm thick pieces and place in your bowl. Very thinly slice the remaining apples and use a potato peeler to cut thin ribbons of the remaining half of the cucumber. Arrange these on top of the trout and scatter over the smoked almonds. Just before serving, stir the lemon juice into the apple dressing and pour generously over the trout.

Celeriac and apple soup with walnut crumpet

I was at a festival with an incredible food offering, and after walking around trying to decide what to eat, I spotted a tiny crumpet van – the search was over. These walnut crumpets are amazing with a bowl of soup. Make your crumpet batter first as it needs to sit.

SERVES 4

CRUMPET

160g plain flour
1 × 7g sachet instant dried yeast
1 tsp salt
200ml full-fat milk
1 tsp sugar
50g butter
a little sunflower oil

CELERIAC AND APPLE SOUP

2 celeriac (approx 1kg in total), peeled
1 tbsp sunflower oil
2 onions, thinly sliced
1l vegetable stock
100ml double cream
200ml milk
1 Granny Smith apple, quartered and very thinly sliced
1 Pink Lady apple, quartered and very thinly sliced
salt

TO SERVE

45g walnuts, toasted
micro celery leaves

Combine the flour, yeast and salt in a large bowl. Warm the milk to blood temperature, then add the sugar and mix with a fork until fully incorporated. Whisk the milk into the flour until you have a smooth batter, then cover with cling film and leave at room temperature until it's doubled in size, about 30 minutes.

Square off one of the celeriacs, keeping all the trim. Cut enough 1cm dice to garnish four bowls of soup – you want a small handful of dice for each bowl. Blanch the celeriac dice in boiling, salted water for a couple of minutes until tender, then drain and set aside.

Roughly chop all the remaining celeriac. In a medium-sized pot over a medium heat, add the oil and the sliced onions. Season with a good pinch of salt and cook until soft and transparent. Add in the chopped celeriac and sweat for a few more minutes, until it is just starting to soften. Pour over the vegetable stock and simmer until the celeriac is very soft, about 15 minutes.

Add in the cream and milk and bring back to a simmer, then take off the heat and blitz the soup with a hand blender until smooth. Taste and add more salt if needed.

When you're nearly ready to eat, cook the crumpet. Melt the butter with a little oil in a 25cm frying pan, and then pour in the crumpet batter. Cook on a medium heat for about 6 minutes, until bubbles start to appear on the uncooked side and the base looks golden. With a spatula, flip the crumpet over and cook for another 6 minutes on the other side.

Allow the crumpet to cool slightly and cut into quarters. Set aside 4 of the toasted walnuts, and finely grate the rest of them over the crumpet.

Warm the soup and ladle into bowls, then garnish with the blanched celeriac dice and apple slices. Break up the reserved walnuts and scatter over each bowl, then finish with micro celery leaves.

Fish finger sandwich

You can't go wrong with a fish finger sandwich. And you certainly can't go wrong when the fish is coated in breadcrumbs and yeast flakes.

SERVES 4

ROAST GARLIC MAYO
3 bulbs of garlic
200g mayonnaise (page 280)

SQUASH AND CELERIAC SLAW
200g butternut squash, peeled and grated
200g celeriac, peeled and grated
10g wakame powder
fine salt

FISH FINGERS
4 large sole fillets
40g pumpkin seeds
40g fine rolled oats
150g panko breadcrumbs
10g garlic powder
10g onion powder
20g nutritional yeast flakes
2 medium eggs
50g plain flour
salt and freshly ground black pepper

TO SERVE
4 brioche buns, split in half and toasted

vegetable oil for shallow frying

Preheat your oven to 160°c fan.

Make your roast garlic mayo first. Wrap the whole bulbs of garlic loosely in tin foil and pop in the oven for 20 minutes, then turn and cook them for a further 20 minutes, until they are very soft. Leave until they're cool enough to handle, then squeeze the soft garlic cloves out of their skins and squash them to a purée using the side of a knife. Mix them through the mayonnaise.

For the slaw, mix the grated squash and celeriac with the wakame powder and a good pinch of salt.

Now for the fish fingers. Cut each sole fillet into two lengthways, removing any bones. In a food processor, lightly blitz the pumpkin seeds and oats together – don't over blend them as you want a bit of texture. Mix the blitzed mixture with the panko, garlic powder, onion powder and yeast flakes and put it all in a rectangular container that's about the same length as your sole fillets.

Whisk the eggs and pour them into another container, then put the flour into a third one. Line them up next to an empty plate to pop the fish on once it's breaded. Lightly season the sole fillets, then coat each side in flour, dusting off any excess. Dip each fillet in the egg, then press them into the panko mix, making sure they're completely covered.

Heat about 100ml vegetable oil in a frying pan on a medium heat. When the oil is hot, fry the fillets in batches for about 2 minutes on each side until golden brown, then drain on kitchen roll. Build up your sandwich: slaw first, then a couple of pieces of fish, and be generous with the mayo!

Devilled lamb kidneys and sweetbreads on toast

There's something quite naughty about having sweetbreads for breakfast!

Traditionally you would start with the kidneys in the pan and then add in the rest of the ingredients, but I find you can control the cooking of the kidneys and sweetbreads better by preparing the sauce in advance (and it's a lot less stressful).

SERVES 4

3 banana shallots, finely diced
45g butter
1 tsp cayenne pepper
1 tsp smoked paprika
50ml brandy
100ml double cream
1 tsp Dijon mustard
1½ tbsp Worcestershire sauce
4 lamb kidneys
200g lamb sweetbreads
10 sprigs of thyme
200ml milk
1 leek
sunflower oil
10g chives, finely chopped
sea salt

TO SERVE
4 slices of sourdough bread, toasted
4 eggs, poached (page 23)

Sauté the diced shallots in 30g of the butter, until they're soft and translucent. Add in the cayenne and paprika and cook for a few minutes, then deglaze with the brandy and reduce until it is almost dry. Add the cream, mustard and Worcestershire sauce, then taste and adjust the seasoning. Set the sauce aside.

Next, prepare the kidneys and sweetbreads. Kidneys have a membrane on the outside that needs to be removed – it peels off easily. Slice the kidney in half lengthways and cut away the white part with scissors or a sharp knife. Cut each half into three pieces.

Place the sweetbreads in a pot with the thyme, milk and a pinch of salt. Gently cook them on a low heat, taking them off the heat just before the milk boils. Strain through a sieve, discarding the milk and thyme, and leave to cool. Sweetbreads also have a membrane that needs to be peeled off (and I find using my fingers is the easiest way).

Season your leek with sea salt and char it either on a very hot griddle pan or on your barbecue until the outer layer is completely black – the intense heat will cook the inside. Allow the leek to cool slightly then peel off and discard the blackened layer, and cut it into four pieces.

To finish it all off, put a little oil into a pan over a high heat. Flash fry the kidneys in the hot pan for 30 seconds, then take them out and put on a plate. In the same hot pan, fry the sweetbreads for a minute to colour, then add the remaining 15g of butter and, once it's foaming, use it to baste the sweetbreads until they're nice and crispy. Return the kidneys to the pan (leaving any juices behind), then add the sauce and the chives and heat it all through.

Spoon the kidneys and sweetbreads on to the toast, add an egg and a piece of leek and devour.

Barbecued chicken thighs with date molasses

These are amazing, I could eat a whole bowl of them.

SERVES 4

200g salt
12 boned chicken thighs
200ml date molasses
20ml rice vinegar
sunflower oil

metal skewers

First make up a brine. Put 200ml water in a small pot with the salt and heat until the salt has dissolved. Pour it into a dish big enough to hold the thighs, and add another 1.8l water. Submerge the chicken thighs in the brine, then set it aside for 30 minutes. This helps keep the chicken moist and seasons it evenly throughout. Pat the brined thighs dry and drain on a wire rack for 30 minutes.

In a small pot, mix the date molasses and vinegar together and reduce slowly on a low heat until it has a syrupy texture.

Skewer and lightly oil the thighs. (I use several skewers to make them easier to turn.) If you're cooking them on a barbecue, wait until the flames have died down and the coals have turned white. Otherwise, heat a griddle pan on high until it's nice and hot. Put the thighs on skin-side down then leave to crisp up for 3 minutes. Flip them on to the meat side and cook for another 2 minutes. Using a pastry brush, coat each side with the molasses mixture and cook for a further 2 minutes on each side (so 4 minutes in total). Turn the heat down slightly if you're cooking them in a griddle pan to stop the molasses from burning.

Brush once more all over and serve, piled high.

Game boudin with polenta

I have only been to Paris once and I was lucky enough to eat in some amazing restaurants. But the sausage and polenta I had in a little backstreet bistro is one of the most memorable dishes I have eaten anywhere.

Using game in the sausage mix works so well with the polenta, and by September and October there's a great selection to choose from. My favourites to use in this boudin are grouse, partridge, venison and hare. Game is very lean, so it's nice to add in a little fat to balance it out. Ask your local butcher to mince you some pork fat, and if that's not available then the same quantity of pork belly works just as well as it has a good percentage of fat in it.

SERVES 4

GAME BOUDIN
sunflower oil
1 medium onion, diced
500g mixed game
200g pork fat, minced
1 tsp allspice
1 tsp cayenne
15g salt

POLENTA
1 medium onion, finely chopped
sunflower oil
60g butter
100g polenta
350–400ml chicken stock
50g Parmesan, grated
   (plus more to serve)

Make your boudin first. In a little oil, sauté the diced onion until transparent and very soft. Either mince or process the game until you have a coarse paste. In a stand mixer with the paddle attachment, mix the minced meat with the fat, allspice, cayenne, cooked onions and salt. You can do it by hand but you'll get a better result in a mixer. Divide the mix into three.

Lay out a sheet of cling film and put a third of the game mix on top. Shape it into a fat sausage about 15cm long, then wrap the cling film around it and use the worktop to tighten the cling film around the meat. Tie off each end and repeat with the remaining game mix so you have three wrapped boudins. Either steam or boil them in simmering water for 15 minutes, then set aside to cool.

For the polenta, sauté the onion in a little oil until soft and transparent. Add half of the butter to the pot, allow it to melt and start browning, then stir in the polenta and toast it for 2 minutes, stirring all the time. Add the chicken stock gradually, stirring frequently, and simmer for 15 to 20 minutes until the polenta is cooked – it should be quite loose so add more stock if needed. Finish with the rest of the butter and grated Parmesan.

Unwrap the boudin and slice on the diagonal into 1cm-thick slices. Pan fry in a little oil until golden brown all over. Serve with the warm polenta and plenty more grated Parmesan and imagine you're in a French café.

Pork belly and black pudding purée

This is one for the meat lovers. Once the pork belly is cooked, you can portion, pan fry and serve it straight away, or you can let it cool and finish it off later. It's easier to portion once it's cooled – you can press it under a board with a little weight on top as it's cooling to get lovely even pieces.

SERVES 4

PORK BELLY

40g salt
1kg pork belly, skin removed
1 tbsp ground cumin
1 tbsp mustard powder
1 tbsp garlic powder
1 tbsp onion powder
½ tbsp cracked black pepper
3 carrots, peeled and chopped into 5cm pieces
3 onions, chopped into 5cm pieces
3 celery sticks, chopped into 5cm lengths
20g thyme
5 fresh bay leaves

1 corn on the cob
50g golden sultanas
50g corn nuts, roughly chopped
200g good-quality black pudding
1 tsp vegetable oil
200ml apple juice
salt and black pepper

First make up a brine for the pork belly. Put 200ml of water in a small pot with the salt and heat until the salt has dissolved. Pour it into a dish big enough to hold the pork belly and add another 1.8 litres water. Submerge the pork belly in the brine, then set it aside for 12 hours. This helps keep the pork moist and seasons it evenly throughout.

Preheat your oven to 160°c fan.

Remove the pork belly from the brine and pat it dry. Mix the cumin, mustard powder, garlic powder, onion powder and black pepper together. Sprinkle the spice mix evenly over both sides of the meat, then rub it in.

Place the carrots, onions and celery in a deep roasting tray and mix through the thyme and bay leaves, then put the pork belly on top. Cover with tin foil and pop it into your oven for 2 to 3 hours, until the meat is soft and tender and almost falling apart. Discard the veg. Season the corn on the cob with salt and pepper and wrap it in tin foil. Put in the oven for about an hour until the corn is tender, turning halfway through the cooking.

While the pork and the corn are cooking, make the black pudding purée. Cut the black pudding into 1cm pieces and, with the oil, sauté in a pot for roughly 2 minutes, until it starts to break up and darken. Add in 150ml of the apple juice. Bring to the boil and reduce until the pan is almost dry and the black pudding has collapsed into a rough, loose purée, stirring regularly to stop it from catching. Blend until smooth, then pass through a sieve and have a taste to see if it needs any seasoning added. Set it aside with a piece of cling film pressed on to the surface of the purée to stop it forming a skin.

Warm the remaining 50ml apple juice and pour over the sultanas. Leave for 15 minutes or so until the sultanas have plumped up. Drain them through a sieve.

Recipe continues overleaf

Once the sweetcorn is cooked, unwrap it from the foil and leave it until it is cool enough to handle, then cut the kernels off the cob.

Portion the cooked pork belly into four pieces. (You can set it aside to cool and press it under a weighted board at this point.)

To finish, gently pan fry the pork in a little oil on all sides until golden brown. Add the sweetcorn to the pan to warm through. In a separate pot, warm the black pudding purée.

Place a piece of pork belly on each plate, and a spoonful of warm black pudding purée next to it. Scatter sultanas, sweetcorn and roughly chopped corn nuts on top of the pork and serve.

Tagliatelle with wild mushrooms and garlic sauce

Use whatever wild mushrooms you can find. My favourites are girolles, pheasant backs and hen of the woods, but this will still be fantastic with some chestnut mushrooms if that's all you can get. This might not look like the quickest recipe to make, but you can make the pasta dough, garlic sauce and crispy capers a few hours in advance and then it's just a matter of bringing it all together at the end.

SERVES 4 (*or 6 as a starter*)

GARLIC SAUCE
200g garlic cloves
300ml double cream

1 recipe pasta dough (page 281)
40g walnuts, toasted
20g butter or oil
200g wild mushrooms, torn into small pieces
1 recipe crispy capers (see below)
1 lemon

I usually make the garlic sauce first, while the pasta dough is resting. Put the peeled garlic cloves in a pot and cover with cold water. Bring to a boil over a high heat, then strain the garlic through a fine sieve and refresh under cold water. Repeat this process two more times, then place the blanched garlic in a small pot and pour over the cream. Let it slowly reduce on a low heat until the cream is just coating the garlic, then blend until smooth and adjust the seasoning if needed. Set aside.

Cut the pasta into two pieces and wrap one of them back up in the cling film. Using a rolling pin, flatten the other piece so it's about 2cm thick, then feed it through the pasta machine on its widest setting. Fold in either end of the pasta sheet so you have a triple layer, then feed it through the machine again. Now, change the pasta machine to the next setting and roll the pasta through twice, without folding it.

Roll it twice through each remaining setting, until it has gone through the second smallest, and you'll end up with a long, thin sheet of pasta. Repeat with the remaining block of pasta.

Once all the pasta is rolled out, fit the tagliatelle attachment on to your machine and carefully feed the sheets through. Dust the tagliatelle in semolina if you're not cooking it straight away to stop it from sticking together.

Set aside two walnuts, then roughly chop the rest.

Blanch the tagliatelle in a pot of salted, simmering water for 2 minutes (add a minute longer if it has dried out a little), then strain it and return to the pan. While the pasta is cooking, heat up the garlic sauce, then mix it through the drained tagliatelle.

In a large frying pan, heat up the butter or oil, then add the mushrooms and sauté them over a medium-high heat for 5 minutes until golden. Mix them through the pasta and divide it between your plates.

Finish each serving with a sprinkling of chopped walnuts and some crispy capers. Finely grate the whole walnuts over the top, then grate over a little lemon zest. Enjoy!

Crispy capers

MAKES 40G

40g lilliput capers
300ml sunflower oil

Fill a deep, narrow pot with 300ml oil and take to 180°c. Strain the capers and pat dry with paper towel. Very carefully fry them in the oil for 3 minutes, then use a slotted spoon to take them out of the oil and into a sieve to drain. Place them on paper towel, changing the paper a couple of times to soak up all the oil.

Whole roasted plaice with seaweed butter, fennel and orange

There is something about serving a whole baked fish to guests that feels both grand and special, but very informal at the same time. This dish is impressive without being over-indulgent. Ask your fishmonger to remove the skin on both sides of the fish.

SERVES 4

1 whole plaice on the bone, weighing about 1.2kg, skin removed
1 fennel bulb
2 easy peeler mandarin oranges
1½ tbsp olive oil
salt and freshly ground black pepper

SEAWEED BUTTER

40g wakame powder
20g yeast flakes, toasted
1½ tbsp lemon juice
1 tsp salt
120g unsalted butter, softened

Preheat your oven to 175°c fan.

Season the plaice and put it on a baking tray. If you want to transfer it to a serving dish once it's cooked, put it on a piece of greaseproof paper that you can lift up once it's cooked. Roast in the oven for 15 to 20 minutes, until just cooked and opaque.

Trim and thinly slice the fennel into a bowl and reserve any of the feathery fronds. With a small, sharp knife cut the peel and pith from the mandarins, then neatly cut out each segment. Add to the sliced fennel in the bowl. With your hands, squeeze the juice from the leftover orange flesh into a small bowl and mix with the olive oil and a pinch of salt. Pour the dressing over the fennel and mandarin segments.

Mix the wakame powder, yeast flakes, lemon juice and salt together and add to the butter, then beat until thoroughly mixed.

Take the cooked fish out of the oven. Immediately spread it with the seaweed butter, then arrange the dressed fennel and orange on top. Garnish with your reserved fennel fronds.

Whole roasted partridge with celeriac and greengages

These ingredients feature on the menu at The Little Chartroom every year without fail – I just love them all together. Both the celeriac compote and the greengage purée are delicious at room temperature, so you can make them in advance and don't have to worry about warming them through when it's time to eat.

SERVES 4

ROASTED PARTRIDGE
4 prepared partridge, weighing about 300g each (pages 18–21)
1 tbsp vegetable oil
100g unsalted butter, diced
1 bunch of thyme
salt

GREENGAGE PURÉE
500g greengages, stoned and quartered
50g sugar
juice of ½ lemon
salt

CELERIAC COMPOTE
1 celeriac, peeled and grated
1 tbsp butter
50g Pommery wholegrain mustard
juice of ½ lemon
salt

Start by getting your partridge out of the fridge. They cook much more evenly at room temperature, so I leave them out on the worktop for an hour before I roast them.

To make the greengage purée, place the quartered greengages in a pot with 50ml water and bring up to a boil. Turn the heat down and add in the sugar and a pinch of salt, then gently simmer until the greengages are soft and the liquid has evaporated. Blend to a smooth purée, then mix in the lemon juice and taste – add a little more lemon juice if it needs it.

Put the grated celeriac in a pot with the butter and a pinch of salt. Cook over a medium heat until the celeriac is tender, then mix through the mustard and the lemon juice. Check the seasoning and adjust if you think it needs it.

Preheat your oven to 175°C fan.

Season the birds with salt. Heat up the oil in a large frying pan – ideally one that can go in the oven – then put in the partridges. Sear them for 6 minutes, turning frequently so they are golden brown all over and making sure that the legs get most of the heat as they take longer to cook. Let the pan cool slightly, then add the butter and put it back on the heat. When the butter starts to foam, add in the thyme and baste the birds for about 30 seconds – spooning the butter over the birds and into the cavity will help them cook evenly.

Move the partridge, breasts up, into the oven. If your pan isn't ovenproof, transfer the birds to a tray, but keep the pan with the buttery cooking juices to baste them when they come out of the oven. Roast for 12 minutes, then baste one more time and leave to rest for at least 10 minutes. Remove the string.

To serve, give everyone a whole partridge with a good dollop of celeriac compote and greengage purée. Drizzle the cooking butter over the partridges – it'll be packed with flavour, with the cooking juices mixed in as well.

Apple and ginger loaf

This has evolved from an amazing carrot cake recipe I got from a friend and colleague when we ran a pub down in England – she made it for Shaun on his birthday and it was the best I'd ever had. This apple and ginger version is equally as good, especially with some blackberry compote and a spoonful of crème fraîche on the side. The berries for the compote need to be frozen overnight and then thawed gently at room temperature with some sugar. It's a wonderfully simple and delicious way to make a compote, and it helps the fruit keep its shape.

SERVES 6–8

2 Granny Smith apples, peeled and cored
170g self-raising flour
1 tsp baking powder
1 tsp bicarbonate of soda
85g dark soft brown sugar
85g caster sugar
1 tbsp ground ginger
3 medium eggs
160g sunflower oil
4 stem ginger bulbs, finely chopped
75g root ginger, peeled and finely grated

TO SERVE
40g butter
40g caster sugar
1 recipe blackberry compote
90g crème fraîche

20 × 12 × 6cm loaf tin, lined with greaseproof paper

To make the cake, first preheat your oven to 175°C fan.

Grate the peeled apples using the largest holes of the grater.

Sift the flour, baking powder and bicarb into a large bowl, then add the dark brown and caster sugars and the ground ginger. Make sure everything is evenly mixed. In a small bowl, whisk the eggs with the sunflower oil. Add to the dry ingredients and mix thoroughly, then stir through the grated apple, chopped stem ginger and grated root ginger.

Pour the batter into the lined loaf tin and bake for 45 minutes to an hour, or until a skewer comes out clean. Allow to cool in the tin, then transfer to a wire rack.

To serve, cut the cake into 3cm slices. Melt the butter in a frying pan, then sprinkle the cake slices with the caster sugar and fry on a medium-high heat until golden in colour on each side.

Serve with the blackberry compote and a spoonful of crème fraîche.

Blackberry Compote

MAKES 360G

300g blackberries
60g caster sugar

The day before you make the loaf, start on the compote. Halve or quarter the blackberries (depending on how big they are) and freeze them overnight. The next day, transfer them to a tray and mix the sugar thoroughly through the berries. Leave to defrost at room temperature, mixing occasionally, until defrosted.

Greengage frangipane tart

Greengages are one of my favourite plums – sweet, juicy and perfect in a frangipane tart! If you don't have enough of them to make the purée, you can spread a thick layer of plum jam on to the base of the tart before filling with the frangipane. And you can of course use plums if you miss the greengage season.

SERVES 8–10

1 recipe sweet pastry (page 282), rested
1 egg, beaten
350g greengages, stoned and halved
70g flaked almonds
50g demerara sugar
150g smooth plum jam
400g clotted cream

GREENGAGE PURÉE
500g greengages, stoned and quartered
50g sugar
juice of ½ lemon
salt

FRANGIPANE
150g caster sugar
100g butter, softened
3 eggs
100g ground almonds
50g plain flour
salt

25cm tart case with a removable base

Roll out your sweet pastry to 5mm thick and carefully line your tart case, leaving a little pastry hanging over the edge (which will get trimmed after it's cooked). Cover the pastry with a double layer of cling film, which also overhangs the edges, then fill with ceramic baking beans. Rest in the fridge for 30 minutes.

Whilst your sweet pastry is resting you can start the greengage purée. Place the greengages in a pot with 50ml water and bring up to a boil, then turn the heat down and add in the sugar and a pinch of salt. Gently simmer until the greengages are soft and the liquid has evaporated. Blend to a smooth purée, add in the lemon juice and taste – add a little more lemon juice if it needs it.

Preheat your oven to 175°c fan.

Bake the pastry case for 15 to 20 minutes, until the base stops looking raw. Carefully remove the baking beans and cling film, then return the tart to the oven for a further 5 minutes, until it is golden brown. Brush the base and sides of the pastry case with a little of the beaten egg and return to the oven for 2 minutes, then set it aside to cool in the tin.

Turn the oven down to 160°c fan.

For the frangipane, cream the sugar and butter together until light and fluffy. Beat in the eggs, one at a time, until they are fully mixed. In another bowl, stir the ground almonds and flour together with a pinch of salt, then fold them into your butter mix until fully incorporated.

When the pastry case is completely cool, use a veg peeler to trim off any pastry that's hanging over the side. Spread a layer of greengage purée over the bottom, then spread the frangipane on top. Push the halved greengages slightly into the frangipane, then sprinkle over the flaked almonds and demerara sugar. Bake for 30 to 35 minutes until the filling is firm and a skewer inserted into the middle comes out clean. Carefully remove the tart from the tin and put it on a flat plate.

Warm the plum jam and brush it thickly over the top of the tart. Cut into slices and serve with a large dollop of clotted cream.

Blackberry cheesecake brownie

Fudgy chocolate brownie with zingy, fresh blackberries and creamy cheesecake – heaven.

SERVES 8

BROWNIE
110g 70% dark chocolate, roughly chopped
110g unsalted butter, cubed
2 medium eggs
170g light soft brown sugar
1 vanilla pod or 1 tsp vanilla extract
75g plain flour
¼ tsp salt

BLACKBERRY CHEESECAKE
500g blackberries
225g cream cheese
2 tbsp icing sugar, sifted
2 tbsp double cream
¾ platinum gelatine leaf

TO FINISH
25g white chocolate

20cm springform cake tin, lined with greaseproof paper

Preheat the oven to 180°c fan.

Make the brownie base first. In a bain-marie, melt the chocolate and butter, then set aside. In a bowl, whisk the eggs, sugar and vanilla together and then, off the heat, beat them into the chocolate mix.

Fold in the flour and salt, then pour the batter into the lined cake tin and bake for 20 minutes until you see cracks at the edges. Leave the brownie to cool in its tin.

Set aside 100g of the blackberries, then blitz the rest of them in a small blender until smooth (a stick blender will also work). Push them through a sieve to get a purée, then weigh out 225g and set aside. In a bowl, whisk the cream cheese, icing sugar and cream together until everything is combined and smooth.

Bloom the gelatine in a small bowl of cold water for 5 minutes. In a small pan, warm the weighed out blackberry purée. Squeeze out any excess water from your gelatine leaf, then add the softened leaf to the purée. Stir until it has dissolved, then beat the purée into the cream cheese mix until it is fully incorporated. Quickly pour it on to the cooled brownie so you have a nice, flat layer, then put it into the fridge to set for a few hours.

To serve, halve the remaining blackberries and decorate the top of the cheesecake with them, then grate over plenty of white chocolate.

Spiced pumpkin and coffee panna cotta

A pumpkin spiced latte is one of my guilty pleasures and inspired this dessert: it would have been rude not to share it with you.

SERVES 4

300g pumpkin or butternut squash, peeled and deseeded
1 tsp sunflower or vegetable oil
70ml whole milk
1 tbsp instant coffee granules
2 leaves platinum gelatine
195ml double cream
50g caster sugar
¼ tsp ground cinnamon
¼ tsp ground nutmeg
¼ tsp ground ginger

TO FINISH

2 tbsp feuilletine flakes
1 tsp cocoa nibs

four 6cm dariole moulds

Chop the peeled pumpkin into small pieces and place into a pot with the oil. Cover with a lid and gently cook on a medium heat, stirring occasionally, until you can easily pierce the pumpkin with a fork, about 5 minutes or so.

Once cooked, remove the lid and keep cooking the pumpkin on a low heat to dry it out a little, stirring frequently to stop it from burning. Blitz to get a smooth purée, then pass it through a sieve and weigh out 50g to use in the panna cotta. Press a bit of cling film on to the surface to stop it forming a skin.

Warm the milk and coffee granules in a small pot until steaming. Bloom the gelatine in a small bowl of cold water for about 5 minutes. Add the weighed out pumpkin purée to the milky coffee along with the cream, sugar, cinnamon, nutmeg and ginger. Stir over a low heat until the sugar has dissolved and the spices are mixed in, then take the pot off the heat.

Squeeze out any excess liquid from the gelatine, then add it to the pot and stir until it has dissolved. Strain the mix into a bowl through a piece of muslin – you might have to squeeze the last bit through but it's worth doing to get a really smooth panna cotta – and put the bowl over ice to cool. Stir the mix regularly to stop the spices all sinking to the bottom and then, once it has cooled but before it sets, divide the panna cotta between your dariole moulds. Put them in the fridge to set for at least 2 hours.

Fill a small bowl with hot but not boiling water and dip the moulds in for 10 seconds, being careful not to get any water in the panna cotta. This should loosen them enough that you can turn the panna cottas out on to serving plates. Sprinkle a little feuilletine and some cocoa nibs on top of each one and serve.

Autumn dinner party menu

The days get shorter again, and the shadows grow longer – a real sign that the seasons are changing. These are the perfect dishes to welcome autumn to your table. They are all designed so you can enjoy the party and not be stuck in the kitchen: most elements can be prepped in advance and organised so there's very little to finish before serving. I am particularly proud of the Paris-Brest – it took a few attempts to get a recipe I was finally happy with but it's very special and I hope you get as much satisfaction out of making it as I do.

Light yet flavoursome venison tartare to start

―――

A big, meaty piece of cod with mussels and pancetta for the table to share

―――

And a show-stopping hazelnut and chocolate Paris-Brest to wrap things up.

Damson negroni

The beautiful, burgundy, autumnal hues make this the perfect drink to start a dinner party! You do need to make the damson gin at least 4 weeks in advance, but it's so simple to make and can be used for many other drinks as well. At a pinch, you can also buy it ready made.

SERVES 6

150ml damson gin
150ml Campari
150ml sweet vermouth
plenty of ice
1 orange

Pour the damson gin, Campari and sweet vermouth into a cocktail tin or mixing glass. Add some ice and stir.

Put some ice into your glasses, then pour over the negroni, putting about 75ml in each glass.

Using a peeler, cut nice big strips of zest from the orange and squeeze them over each glass to release the oils. You can either garnish each drink with the zest or discard it.

Damson gin

It's best to stone the damsons as they can taint the taste of the finished gin, but a cherry stoner does the job very easily.

MAKES 1.25L

500g damsons
250g caster sugar
1l gin

2l Kilner jar

Wash the damsons, then remove the stems and stone them. Place the damsons and sugar in the Kilner jar and shake so it is thoroughly mixed. Pour over the gin and seal the jar.

For the next 5 to 7 days, shake the jar daily until the sugar has all dissolved, then store in a dry, dark place for a minimum of 4 weeks and a maximum of 3 months. The longer you store it, the better the flavour will be.

Pass the gin through a muslin cloth and store in clean bottles.

Venison tartare with smoked celeriac remoulade

Smoking the remoulade is optional here, but I think it works well with the gamey venison. You just need to get some smoking chips and a smoking tube, or alternatively you could make your mayonnaise with a smoked rapeseed oil.

SERVES 6

SMOKED CELERIAC REMOULADE
1 large (approx. 800g) celeriac, peeled and grated
juice of ½ lemon
2 tsp sea salt
100g mayonnaise (page 280)
20g Pommery mustard
10g chives, finely chopped

VENISON TARTARE
150g shimeji mushrooms
200ml pickle liquor (page 280)
80g cornichons
300g venison haunch or fillet
1 tbsp good-quality olive oil
2 tsp sea salt
25g buckwheat, toasted

6 slices of sourdough bread

For the remoulade, mix the grated celeriac with the lemon juice and salt and leave for 10 minutes until it has wilted slightly. Add the mayonnaise, Pommery mustard and finely chopped chives and stir through so everything is well mixed. If you're smoking the remoulade, smoke it for 15 minutes according to the instructions on page 22.

Next, make the tartare. Using scissors, trim the shimeji mushrooms, leaving about 1cm of the stalk on and put them in a bowl. Warm 100ml of the pickle liquor and pour it over the mushrooms. Set aside to cool.

Half the cornichons lengthways, then cut into thin slices about 2 or 3mm thick.

Trim any sinew off the venison and discard, then cut the meat into 1cm dice and put it into a bowl. Mix the remaining pickle liquor with the olive oil and stir it through the diced venison. Add the salt, taste and add a little more if needed.

Strain the pickled shimejis through a sieve. Spread a generous amount of celeriac remoulade on your serving plate. Cover it with the venison, then scatter over the cornichons, pickled shimejis and toasted buckwheat.

Chargrill the sourdough and serve alongside the tartare.

Baked cod with mussels, pancetta, cider and sage

I love to salt or brine fish as it helps it retain its moisture and seasons the fish throughout. It makes sense to do this in the morning as your fish will need to dry a little after brining. I tend to prep the mussels at the same time and then pop them in the fridge until I need them. The dish itself takes no time to put together.

SERVES 6

100g fine salt
1.2kg side of cod, skin on
3kg mussels
1 tbsp vegetable oil
250g pancetta lardons
4 garlic cloves, thinly sliced
500ml cider
200ml double cream
4 sprigs of sage, picked and roughly chopped

a large, deep ovenproof dish that can fit the cod in as a whole piece

First make the brine. Heat 200ml water in a small pot, then add the salt and mix until it has dissolved. Pour this into a large container, then add the remaining 1.8l water. Put the fish into the brine and make sure it's completely submerged, then leave for 30 minutes. Transfer the fish to a wire rack and pop in the fridge for a couple of hours to dry.

Wash and remove the beards from the mussels and discard any that aren't fully closed. Pop them in the fridge until you need them.

Preheat the oven to 175°c fan.

Line your ovenproof dish with a sheet of greaseproof paper and place the cod, skin-side down, on top. Bake the fish for 6 minutes, then gently flip it over so the skin is facing up and bake for a further 6 minutes.

When the cod has almost finished cooking, heat the oil in a large pot over a medium heat. Add the pancetta lardons and sauté until they start to colour, then add the garlic, mussels and cider. Cover the pot with a lid and cook for about 2 minutes until the mussels have opened (but discard any that stubbornly stay closed). Finish by adding the cream and sage.

Once the cod is cooked, gently peel off its skin and remove the greaseproof paper underneath it. Scatter over the mussels and pancetta and their cooking liquor and serve.

Autumn vegetable gratin

The colours and flavours in this gratin are absolutely beautiful. To make timings easier, I usually cook it in the afternoon, then just warm it through in the oven for 20 minutes at the same time as I'm cooking the fish.

SERVES 6

200g Maris Piper potatoes, peeled
200g butternut squash, peeled and deseeded
200g beetroot, peeled
200g celeriac, peeled
750ml double cream
3 bay leaves
a small bunch of thyme
salt

25 × 20cm rectangle oven dish

Preheat your oven to 160°c fan.

Using a Japanese mandolin, thinly slice the potatoes, squash, beetroot and celeriac, keeping them all separate. You can also do this with a knife, but a mandolin means you get very even slices. Season lightly with salt.

Heat the cream with the bay leaves, thyme and 2 teaspoons of salt until it is steaming.

Make a layer with half the potato slices in the base of your dish, then make a layer with half the beetroot on top, then half the butternut squash, then half the celeriac. Repeat until all the vegetables have been used. Pass the hot cream through a sieve, then pour it over the vegetables – there should be enough that you have about a finger's width of cream above the vegetables.

Bake for 1 to 1½ hours, until a knife goes through the vegetables with no resistance.

Chicory salad with chestnuts and pumpkin seeds

A crisp salad, the perfect foil to the creamy gratin. The pumpkin seed purée can be made the day before, leaving very little to do when it's time to eat.

SERVES 6

PUMPKIN SEED PURÉE
150g pumpkin seeds
150g butter
280g whole milk
1 garlic clove
90g sunflower oil
2 tsp white wine vinegar
1 tbsp lemon juice
salt

CHICORY SALAD
30g chestnuts, cooked and peeled
4 chicory
juice of ½ lemon
2 tbsp extra virgin olive oil
sea salt

Get started with the pumpkin seed purée. Keeping the temperature low so the butter doesn't burn, toast the pumpkin seeds in the butter until golden brown, about 4 to 5 minutes. Strain the seeds through a sieve over a bowl and season them with a good pinch of salt. Keep the butter and put 30g of toasted seeds to one side.

Place the rest of the pumpkin seeds in a bowl with the milk, cover with cling film and sit them over a pot of simmering water for 1 hour. Transfer the contents of the bowl to a blender and blitz with the garlic, oil and vinegar until smooth. Season to taste with the lemon juice and salt.

Roughly chop the chestnuts and add them to a pan with the butter that you used to toast the pumpkin seeds. Toast them on a low heat for 2 minutes, then strain through a sieve and season with a pinch of salt.

Separate the chicory leaves and arrange them on a plate, then pop them in the fridge until needed. In a small bowl, mix the lemon juice with the olive oil and a good pinch of salt.

When you're ready to serve, just sprinkle a pinch of sea salt over the chicory leaves, then dress them with the lemon dressing. Drizzle over the pumpkin seed purée and finish with the toasted chestnuts and pumpkin seeds.

Hazelnut and chocolate Paris-Brest

This dessert has quite a few components and is an absolute showstopper.

It's better if you make everything apart from the choux pastry the day before. The extra time allows it all to set and rest properly, and it'll make life easier – all you'll need to do is put it together.

If your guests are coming in the evening, cook the choux around lunchtime so you allow time for it to cool before finishing and assembling the Paris-Brest.

SERVES 6

CHOCOLATE CREMEUX
3 tsp caster sugar
3 egg yolks
95ml double cream
75ml full-fat milk
125g milk chocolate drops
35g dark chocolate drops

HAZELNUT PRALINE CHANTILLY
260ml double cream
1 platinum gelatine leaf
50g milk chocolate drops
50g praline paste
salt

CHOCOLATE FRANGIPANE
50g dark chocolate, roughly chopped
50g caster sugar
50g butter, softened
1 medium egg
50g ground almonds

CRAQUELIN
40g plain flour
40g caster sugar
40g cold butter, cubed

CHOUX PASTRY
50g milk
50g butter
½ tsp caster sugar
50g plain flour
1½ medium eggs, beaten (about 75g)
salt

TO FINISH
30g blanched hazelnuts, toasted and roughly chopped
20g praline pieces, roughly chopped
20g cocoa nibs

Make the cremeux, Chantilly, frangipane and craquelin the day before.

To make the chocolate cremeux, put the sugar and egg yolks in a bowl and whisk together until pale. In a heavy-bottomed pan, heat the cream and milk until steaming. Pour it in a thin stream into the egg mix, whisking all the time, then transfer the lot back to the pan. Cook over a medium-low heat, stirring continuously, until the cremeux reaches 83°C and coats the back of the spoon. Remove from the heat and mix in both the milk and dark chocolate drops, stirring until they have completely melted and you have a thick, glossy cremeux. Pour into a container and allow to cool, then place in the fridge and leave to set overnight.

For the hazelnut praline Chantilly, put the double cream into a large pot with a pinch of salt and bring it to a boil. Bloom the gelatine in some cold water for about 5 minutes. Put the milk chocolate drops and praline paste into a bowl and pour over the hot cream. Whisk until they have melted completely, then squeeze any excess water from the gelatine leaf and add it to the chocolate cream. Stir until it has completely dissolved, then give it a blitz with an immersion blender to make sure everything is mixed and emulsified. Pour the praline Chantilly into a container and leave to set in the fridge overnight.

For the chocolate frangipane, melt the chocolate in a bain-marie. In a bowl, beat the sugar and butter together until light and fluffy, then add the egg and beat until fully incorporated. Fold in the ground almonds and then stir in the melted chocolate. Set the frangipane aside to cool, then transfer it to a piping bag (you don't need a nozzle) and pop it into the fridge overnight.

To make the craquelin, put the flour, sugar and butter in a bowl and rub it together with your fingers to form a dough. Put the dough between two sheets of greaseproof paper and roll to about 5mm thick, then put it into the fridge overnight.

The next morning, transfer the hazelnut Chantilly to a bowl and whisk until it's thick and pipeable, then put it into a piping bag with a large (about 1cm) star nozzle and pop it back in the fridge again for at least an hour to firm up.

At about lunchtime, make the choux pastry. Preheat your oven to 175°c fan and line a baking tray with greaseproof paper. Using a dark marker pen, draw a circle 10cm in diameter on the greaseproof and then turn the paper over on the tray – you should still be able to see the circle.

To make the choux pastry, put the milk, butter and sugar in a pot with 50ml water and a pinch of salt and bring to the boil. Remove the pot from the heat while you mix in the flour, then return it to a high heat and cook, stirring furiously, until you have a thick, smooth dough that comes away from the side of the pan. Leave the dough to cool (or for speed you can transfer it to a stand mixer and, using the paddle attachment, beat until the mix has cooled). Once it's cool, gradually add the beaten eggs, mixing until they are fully incorporated and you have a tight, shiny choux dough.

Transfer the dough to a piping bag with an 18mm plain nozzle. Using the circle you drew earlier as a guide, pipe a large circle with an inside diameter of 10cm on to the lined baking tray. Pipe another two layers of choux dough on top so you have a ring about 3cm high, then neaten it up by smoothing the inside with a wet finger.

Now, get your sheet of craquelin out of the fridge and, using a 14cm and a 7cm bowl as guides, cut out a ring of dough. (Any leftover craquelin can be rolled out again between two sheets of greaseproof and frozen.) Place the craquelin carefully on top of the choux (you want it to completely coat the choux as it cooks), then bake for 35 minutes. Get your chocolate frangipane out of the fridge to come to room temperature so it softens enough to pipe. If it's still a little stiff, use your hands to warm it up.

When the choux ring is finished baking, leave it to cool on a wire rack but keep the oven on. Once the choux ring has completely cooled, carefully cut it in half horizontally and set the top aside. Pipe chocolate frangipane into the base and bake for 10 to 12 minutes, until the frangipane is firm to the touch. Leave to cool on a wire rack – it must be completely cool before finishing, as otherwise the cremeux and Chantilly will melt. While it cools, get your cremeux out of the fridge to warm up a bit, and after 30 minutes transfer it to a piping bag with a 1cm plain nozzle.

To finish, pipe the chocolate cremeux in fat drops on top of the frangipane, alternating with rosettes of praline Chantilly. Sprinkle half of each of the toasted hazelnuts, praline pieces and cocoa nibs over the cremeux and Chantilly. Gently balance the top half of the choux ring on top, then decorate with more cremeux and Chantilly. Sprinkle with the remaining hazelnuts, praline and cocoa nibs.

Put your Paris-Brest in the fridge until 30 minutes before serving, but don't leave it there for longer than 4 hours as the choux will go soft. Let it come up to room temperature before wowing everyone in the room.

Winter

Winter is as much about the style of the food as the produce – saucy ragus, creamy spuds, broths, soups, pies, braised meat and root vegetables. All so warm and comforting when it's cold and wet outside.

Oysters with jalapeño hot sauce

Sweet, salty, spicy – incredible!

SERVES 4

JALAPEÑO HOT SAUCE
60g fresh jalapeños, roughly chopped
60g gherkins, roughly chopped
50g sugar
25ml pickle liquor (page 280)
20ml cider vinegar

8 oysters, shucked (page 10)

First make the hot sauce. Put the roughly chopped jalapeños into a blender with the gherkins, sugar, pickle liquor and cider vinegar and blend until you have a smooth sauce.

Spoon a little of the hot sauce on to each oyster.

Ox tongue and Cheddar cheese soldiers

Ox tongue sandwiches and soup were a regular favourite at my grandparents', and I wanted to make something similar for the restaurant lunch menu: so the ox tongue soldier was created! The perfect dipper but also amazing by itself.

SERVES 4

1 ox tongue
2 carrots, peeled and roughly chopped
1 onion, roughly chopped
4 bay leaves
30g fine salt
20g thyme
4 slices of sourdough bread
50g butter
200g good-quality Cheddar, coarsely grated

Place the ox tongue in a pot and cover with cold water. Bring to a boil, then strain through a colander and rinse the tongue under the cold tap. Put it back into the pot and cover with fresh, cold water, then add the chopped carrots, onion, bay and salt. Set aside a few sprigs of the thyme and put the rest in the pot. Bring to a simmer and cook for 3 to 4 hours, until the tongue is tender and a knife goes through it easily.

Remove the cooked tongue from the pot and set it aside until it's just cool enough to handle. Peel off the skin and discard – it should peel away easily as long as it is still warm. You can also use a knife to cut it away. Cut about half of the tongue into thin slices (and you can freeze the leftovers).

Preheat your grill to high.

Pick the thyme leaves from the reserved sprigs of thyme. Spread your bread with butter and grill on both sides. Put a generous layer of tongue slices on the grilled bread, cover with grated Cheddar and put them back under the grill until the cheese has melted and started to brown in places. Cut into soldiers and sprinkle over the picked thyme leaves.

Haggis sausage roll and turnip ketchup

This is a classic flavour combo and very easy to make. You'll have some leftover haggis, but you can freeze any excess or double the pastry recipe to make lots of sausage rolls for a party.

I make these with the rough puff pastry on page 282, but shop-bought puff pastry is great if you don't have time to make your own – just use two sheets of the ready-rolled kind.

MAKES 8 (*or 16 party-size*)

HAGGIS
1 lamb pluck
1 tsp sunflower oil
1 onion, finely diced
1 tbsp allspice
1 tsp cayenne
1 tsp salt
1 tsp black pepper
50g pinhead oatmeal
150g lamb mince

1 recipe rough puff pastry (page 282)
2 egg yolks, beaten with a splash of milk
1 tbsp sesame seeds
1 tsp cumin seeds
1 tsp nigella seeds

Start with the haggis. Place the lamb pluck in a pot and cover with cold water. Gently bring to a simmer, then skim off any impurities and cook for 30 minutes.

Remove the cooked pluck from the pot with a slotted spoon and set aside to cool. Measure out 500ml of the cooking liquor and set it aside for later.

Cut the offal – the heart, lungs and liver – from the pluck. Feel through for any tubes, bits of white cartilage or windpipe and discard, then remove and discard the small sac on the liver. Mince or finely chop the offal – you want a finished weight of 400g.

In a frying pan with the oil, sweat down the onion until soft and transparent. Add in the allspice, cayenne, salt, pepper and oats and cook for 1 minute, then stir in the 500ml reserved cooking liquor and gently cook until the oats are soft.

Add the lamb mince and finely chopped offal to the frying pan and cook for 20 minutes. Taste and add more seasoning if necessary. Remove the haggis from the pan and leave it to cool completely, then place in the fridge for an hour to firm up.

Using a little flour, roll one of the pieces of pastry to a rectangle about 40 × 20cm and 4mm thick, with the long side nearest to you. Take some of the haggis and put it in a thick line about 4cm thick along the middle of the pastry. Fold the bottom of the pastry over the filling and mould it with your hands to get a nice, neat finish, then trim off the excess, leaving a lip of about 3cm where the pastry edges join. Use a fork to crimp the edges together. Repeat with the other block of pastry and the remaining haggis, then liberally egg wash both rolls and leave to sit for 10 minutes.

Preheat the oven to 180°C fan.

Egg wash both the rolls again and sprinkle with the sesame, cumin and nigella seeds, then place them on a lined baking tray. Bake in the oven for 20 minutes, until they are golden brown all over.

Cut each roll into four sausage rolls and serve alongside a dollop of turnip ketchup – I like to warm it up a little bit first.

Turnip ketchup

This makes more than you need but it will keep in a jar in the fridge for a week.

MAKES 500ML

1 tbsp vegetable or sunflower oil
1 onion, sliced
600g yellow turnip (or swede), peeled and roughly chopped
1 garlic clove, finely chopped
50g dark soft brown sugar
1 tbsp black treacle
2 tsp cider vinegar
salt

Put the oil in a pot with a lid and put over a medium heat. Add the onion and a pinch of salt, sauté until soft, then stir in the chopped turnip and garlic and sauté for 2 to 3 minutes. Cover and cook over a low heat until the turnip is tender. Add the sugar, treacle and vinegar and cook until there is no liquid left and everything is very soft.

Blend to a smooth purée, then taste and adjust the seasoning.

Smoked duck and beetroot salad

Duck meat takes on smoke really well, so this is a great place to use the hot smoking technique on page 22.

SERVES 4

200g golden beetroot
200g red beetroot
100ml pickle liquor (page 280)
2 duck breasts, smoked (page 22)
100g mixed baby leaves
sea salt

DRESSING

juice of 1 orange
1 tbsp cold-pressed rapeseed oil
1 tsp red wine vinegar
fine salt

Preheat your oven to 175°c fan.

Wrap one golden and one red beetroot in tin foil and bake for about an hour – the size of the beetroot will determine how long it'll take to cook; you can check if it's done by inserting a skewer into it. If there's any resistance it needs a little longer. Once the beetroots are cooked, allow them to cool enough to handle, then rub the skin off. (It should rub away easily if they're still a little warm.) Cut into bite-sized pieces.

Peel and thinly slice the remaining beetroots and put them in a bowl. Heat up the pickle liquor then pour it over the beetroots and leave until it has cooled to room temperature.

Next make the dressing, whisking together the orange juice, rapeseed oil, vinegar and a pinch of salt.

Take the smoked duck breasts and put them, skin-side down, in a cold pan. Cook on a medium heat for 5 minutes, then turn them over and cook for 2 minutes on the other side. Remove the duck from the pan and rest for 5 minutes, then slice.

Dress the baby leaves with a pinch of sea salt and the orange dressing. Build the salad on your plates, with pieces of cooked beetroot, smoked duck breast, pickled beetroot and salad leaves.

Radicchio and orange salad

Bitter, sweet, crunchy, creamy – this salad is perfect by itself or as an accompaniment to a larger dish. Douglas fir is a pine needle that has incredible citrussy notes. It makes a fantastic vinegar that marries perfectly with the orange in this salad.

SERVES 4

2 tbsp buckwheat
1 orange
1 tbsp Douglas fir vinegar (page 276) or white wine vinegar
½ tbsp cold-pressed rapeseed oil
1 radicchio
1 recipe fresh cheese (page 280)
sea salt

Toast the buckwheat in a dry frying pan over a medium heat, moving continuously.

Using a small, sharp, serrated knife, cut the skin off the orange, making sure there's no pith left. Cut out the individual segments over a bowl to catch all the juice, discarding any pips or bits of membrane. Squeeze any last bits of juice from the leftovers.

Pass the orange juice through a fine sieve, then mix with the vinegar, rapeseed oil and a pinch of salt to taste.

Tear the leaves from the base of the radicchio, then cut them in half and put in a bowl. Dress with the orange dressing and more sea salt if you think it needs it.

Build the salad on individual plates, layering the radicchio with orange segments and fresh cheese and finishing with a generous sprinkling of toasted buckwheat.

Curried mussel soup

The perfect winter warmer with a little kick. Mussels are delicious but sometimes you just want to eat them without messing about with the shells, so this is ideal.

SERVES 4

- 2kg live mussels
- 400ml white wine
- 4 banana shallots, thinly sliced
- 2 garlic cloves, thinly sliced
- 2 tbsp sunflower oil
- 2 tbsp Madras curry powder
- 150ml double cream
- 70g carrots, peeled and cut into 5mm dice
- 120g celeriac, trimmed, peeled and cut into 5mm dice
- 1 tbsp olive oil
- salt

Rinse the mussels in cold water and pull out their beards. Discard any that aren't tightly closed.

Put a large pot with a lid on a high heat, and when it's good and hot throw in the mussels and white wine and cover with the lid. Cook for about 2 minutes, until all the mussels have opened. Strain through a colander, keeping the cooking liquor, and set aside to cool a little. Remove the mussels from the shells, discarding any that have refused to open, and set 20 of the nicest ones aside to garnish the soup.

Over a medium heat, sweat the shallots and garlic down in the sunflower oil, and add a pinch of salt. When they're nice and soft, stir in the Madras curry powder and cook gently for 5 minutes. The spices will soak up the oil, so add a little more if it is looking too dry. Add the mussels and 500ml of the cooking liquor and bring to a simmer, then pour in the cream and simmer once more. Transfer everything to a blender and blitz until the soup is very smooth, then pass it through a sieve, taste and adjust the seasoning if needed.

Sauté the diced carrot and celeriac in a frying pan with the olive oil and a pinch of salt until tender and lightly browned.

Put any of the remaining cooking liquor in a small pot and add the reserved mussels, then warm them over a low heat.

Heat up the soup and pour it into bowls, then garnish with the sautéed veg and some of the warmed mussels.

Ham hock broth

I love making broths; I always make a good amount to last a few days. They're great for lunch or dinner with lots of crusty bread to dunk in.

SERVES 4

1 smoked ham hock
3 garlic cloves
10g thyme
1 bay leaf
200g pearl barley
140g turnip (or swede), peeled and cut into 5mm dice
6 spring onions, sliced

Place the ham hock in a deep pot and cover with plenty of cold water. Bring to a simmer, then strain off the water. Add 3l of fresh water and the garlic, thyme and bay leaf and bring back to the boil, then cover with a lid and simmer gently for 4 hours until the meat is tender.

With two slotted spoons, remove the ham from the stock and put it aside until it's cool enough to handle. Pick the meat into small bite-sized pieces, discarding any bone, sinew or cartilage. Pass the stock through a fine sieve and measure 1.5l of it into a clean pot.

Bring the stock to a boil, then add the pearl barley and simmer for 15 minutes. Throw in the diced turnip and cook until it is tender, about 5 minutes. If you like it more brothy, you can add more stock.

When the pearl barley and turnip are cooked, add the spring onions and picked ham hock, warm through and serve.

Crab thermidor muffin

I LOVE this dish! When you add in the cream it might look like the sauce is going to split but don't panic – the egg brings it back together.

SERVES 4

MUFFIN
145ml milk
250g strong bread flour
1 tsp sugar
1 tsp fine salt
1 tsp dry active yeast
1 egg
20g butter, softened
30g semolina

CRAB THERMIDOR
2 shallots, finely diced
sunflower oil
1 tbsp tomato purée
50ml brandy
150ml white wine
150ml fish stock (or ½ fish stock cube in 150ml boiling water)
1 tbsp Dijon mustard
100ml double cream
1 egg yolk
25g Parmesan, finely grated
10g chives, finely chopped
150g picked crab meat (pick through the meat again as there will always be some shell left)

Begin with the muffin dough. In a pot, warm the milk to 35°C. In a large bowl (or a stand mixer with the dough hook), mix the flour, sugar, salt and yeast together. Add the egg and the butter and mix until they're incorporated and you have a breadcrumb consistency, then pour in the warm milk and mix to get a shaggy dough. Knead the dough for 5 to 10 minutes, until it is smooth and elastic. Oil a bowl and pop the dough in, then cover with cling film. Leave to prove at room temperature for 2 hours.

Once the dough has doubled in size, knock it back with your fist, then shape it into a smooth ball. Dust a 26cm cast iron frying pan with a little of the semolina, then put in the dough and dust the top with the rest of the semolina. Push it into the edges of the pan with your fingers. Cover with cling film and leave to prove for 1 to 2 hours, until the dough has doubled in size.

While the dough proves, make the thermidor. Over a medium-high heat, sauté the shallots in a pan with a little oil until they are soft and transparent. Add the tomato purée and cook it for a few minutes, stirring so it doesn't catch, then pour in the brandy and white wine. Bring to a boil and reduce until the pan is almost dry. Add the fish stock and, again, bring to a boil and reduce to almost dry. Stir in the mustard, then add the cream, bring to a boil and reduce it by half. Turn down the heat to medium, then beat in the egg yolk and cook, stirring all the time, for 2 minutes. Finally, add the grated Parmesan and gently mix until it has all melted, then finish with the chopped chives. Mix the picked crab meat through the thermidor sauce so it's well combined. Set aside to cool.

Preheat the oven to 175°c fan. Once the muffin dough has proved, put the pan on a medium-low heat until the muffin is golden brown on the bottom – about 10 minutes. Flip it over and cook for 5 minutes on the other side, then put in the oven for another 10 minutes until baked through and golden brown all over. Turn the muffin out on to a wire rack to cool.

Turn on your grill and put the shelf at least 10cm below the grill. Once the muffin is cool, slice the top crust off (you can use it to make breadcrumbs). Spread with a thick layer of the crab thermidor, then put it under the grill until the sauce is bubbling and caramelised – about 5 minutes. Cut into quarters and serve.

Ham hock rarebit with fried eggs

This is another favourite from our brunch days at The Little Chartroom. You need a good, strong Cheddar for the rarebit – my favourite is St Andrews Farmhouse Cheddar, which you can get from I. J. Mellis.

Another good tip is to always keep the cooking liquid from the ham – it makes a great base for soups, broths and sauces.

SERVES 4

1 smoked ham hock
10g thyme
4 bay leaves
6 garlic cloves
50g butter
50g plain flour
200ml stout
200g Cheddar, grated
50g Pommery mustard
2 tbsp Worcestershire sauce
8 thin-cut slices of sourdough
4 eggs
sunflower oil
5g chives, finely sliced
sea salt and freshly ground black pepper

Place the ham hock in a deep pot and cover with plenty of cold water. Bring to a simmer, then strain off the water. Add fresh water to cover the ham hock and bring it back to the boil, then add the thyme, bay and garlic, turn down the heat to a simmer and cook until the meat is tender and pulls easily away from the bone, about 4 hours.

Take the ham out of the cooking liquid and set it aside until cool enough to handle. With your fingers, pick the meat off the bone, removing any sinew or fat, then shred it into smaller pieces.

In a small pot over a medium heat, melt the butter, letting it brown a bit. Add the flour, and cook for a few minutes, whisking frequently to stop it from catching. Gradually add the stout, whisking continuously, until you have a thick sauce, then finally stir in the grated Cheddar, mustard and Worcestershire sauce.

Toast or grill all the slices of bread on one side only and put them on a baking tray. Spread the untoasted sides with a layer of the rarebit and put them back under the grill for 3 minutes so they are bubbling and caramelised. While they're under the grill, fry the eggs in a little oil.

Scatter a good layer of shredded ham hock on four of the pieces and add some chives, then top with another piece of rarebit toast and then a fried egg. Season with plenty of sea salt and freshly ground black pepper.

White beans and black pudding

This is a real hearty dish. Breakfasty, but also appropriate at dinner time. The beans can be cooked on the day from dry but are better if they are soaked in cold water for 12 hours prior.

SERVES 4

300g dried cannellini beans
2 bulbs of garlic, unpeeled and cut in half
sunflower oil
1l ham stock
4 eggs
200g black pudding, cut into 1cm slices
salt

If you haven't managed to soak the beans, place them in a pot and cover with cold water. Bring to a boil, remove from the heat and let them sit for an hour.

Place the halved garlic bulbs in a pot with a little oil, flesh-side down. Cook until they are lightly caramelised, then add the beans and the ham stock. Bring to a simmer and cook for about 30 minutes, until the beans are soft. Season and taste.

Strain the beans through a sieve, keeping the liquid. Take about a third of the beans and put them in a blender with the squeezed-out garlic cloves. Blitz with enough cooking liquid to give you a loose, smooth purée – add it gradually so you get the perfect consistency. Taste and adjust the seasoning and fold the remaining beans through the purée.

Bring a small pot of water to the boil and carefully place the eggs in. Boil for 5½ minutes, then cool under cold water. Gently crack the shells and peel the skin away.

Pan fry the black pudding in a little oil for 2 minutes on each side, then break it up a bit with a spoon. If you need to, warm the eggs through in a little warm water. Serve the white beans in a bowl with a whole soft-boiled egg on top and scatter the black pudding around the edges.

Cauliflower with vadouvan butter

This is a lovely way to jazz up the humble cauliflower, and it is a great accompaniment to any protein or as a meal in its own right.

SERVES 4

VADOUVAN BUTTER
4 shallots, thinly sliced
4 garlic cloves, thinly sliced
15g fresh ginger, finely chopped
2 tbsp sunflower oil
4 bay leaves
2 strips of orange peel
4 cloves
2 tbsp fennel seeds
2 tbsp cumin seeds
2 tbsp mustard seeds
2 tsp curry powder
2 black cardamom pods,
　crushed with the back of a knife
1 tsp turmeric
½ tsp chilli powder
10 peppercorns
1 tsp salt
250g butter

1 good-sized cauliflower
sunflower oil
1 recipe crispy capers (page 179)
sea salt

Sweat down the shallots, garlic and ginger in a wide pan with the sunflower oil until soft and translucent. Add the bay, orange peel, cloves, fennel, cumin, mustard seeds, curry powder, black cardamom, turmeric, chilli, peppercorns and salt and cook for 10 minutes on a medium-low heat, stirring so the spices don't burn. The spices will soak up the oil, so add another splash if you think it needs it. Turn the heat down to low and add the butter, then cook very, very gently for 30 minutes, stirring to stop anything from catching. Strain through a fine sieve into a bowl and discard the solids.

Cut the cauliflower vertically into as many 1.5–2cm thick steaks as you can. Season both sides with salt and set aside for 10 minutes. Add a little oil to a wide frying pan – enough to cover the base – and add the cauliflower steaks and any stray florets (you might need to do this in batches). Fry until they're tender and golden brown, about 3 minutes on each side, then add three large spoonfuls of vadouvan butter to the pan and let it melt. Cook the cauliflower steaks for another 2 minutes on each side, basting with the melted butter.

Serve with more melted vadouvan poured over the top and a good sprinkling of crispy capers.

Red mullet with langoustine sauce

I still remember the first time I tasted a langoustine bisque – it blew my mind. This dish is all about flavour and letting the produce sing.

Always keep the shells when you eat langoustines and put them in the freezer so you can make this classic sauce. You could also use the same weight of crab or lobster shells – langoustine shells make a sweeter bisque though.

SERVES 4

LANGOUSTINE SAUCE
1kg langoustine shells
sunflower oil
2 carrots, peeled and thinly sliced
1 onion, thinly sliced
1 fennel bulb, trimmed and thinly sliced
50g tomato purée
100ml brandy
500ml fish stock
300ml whole milk
2 star anise
2 fresh bay leaves
½ tsp fennel seeds
½ tsp coriander seeds
100ml double cream
fine salt

4 red mullet fillets

Preheat your oven to 180°c fan.

Put the langoustine shells on a baking tray and roast in the oven for 10 minutes, until brown.

In a pot big enough to take all the shells, add enough sunflower oil to cover the base. Over a medium heat, sweat down the carrots, onion and fennel for 5 minutes, until starting to soften. Stir in the tomato purée and cook for 5 minutes, then add the roasted langoustine shells and mix well. Deglaze with the brandy, stirring so nothing sticks, and reduce until the pan is almost dry. Pour the fish stock and milk into the pan and add the star anise, bay and fennel and coriander seeds. Bring to the boil, then turn down to a simmer and leave to cook for 1 hour.

Add the cream and bring the sauce back to the boil, then immediately take it off the heat and pass through a fine sieve into a smaller pot. Bring to the boil and reduce until the sauce coats the back of the spoon and tastes nice and punchy but not too strong.

Remove any bones left in the red mullet fillets – tweezers work well to take out the pin bones that run down the centre. Drop the pin bones into a small bowl of water to help them come off the end of the tweezer. Sprinkle over a little salt to season.

Put a wide frying pan over a medium heat and add a splash of sunflower oil. Once it's hot, place the red mullet fillets in, skin-side down. Press gently with a fish slice or similar to make sure the skin is flat in the pan and getting crispy. Cook for 2 minutes, then flip over and cook for 30 seconds on the other side. Serve with the langoustine sauce.

Cod and cullen skink

This is a dish that my husband, Shaun, likes to make at home. He loves food – loves eating it, reading about it, serving it – but ironically he hates cooking it! He has a few dishes that he makes and they're mostly one-pan wonders – this one is the best. (He cheekily buys the cullen skink from our local fishmongers.)

SERVES 4

400g smoked haddock fillet
350ml double cream
50ml whole milk
1 tbsp butter
2 garlic cloves, thinly sliced
2 banana shallots, thinly sliced
100ml white wine
200g baby potatoes, cut into bite-sized pieces
6 baby leeks, cut into 1cm pieces
60g baby spinach
10g chives, finely chopped
800g cod
salt

Preheat your oven to 170°C fan.

Using a sharp knife, cut out the central part of the smoked haddock fillet – the bit with the most bones in it – but don't throw it away. Place the rest of the fillet in a pot with the cream and milk and gently warm until it's almost simmering. Take it off the heat and strain through a sieve into another pot. Flake the cooked smoked haddock and set it aside.

Put the reserved bony bit of fish into the strained cooking liquid, then put it back on the heat and simmer very gently for 30 minutes to extract all the flavour.

Melt the butter and then add in the sliced garlic and shallots and gently sauté until soft. Pour in the white wine and reduce until the pan is almost dry, then add the potatoes and sauté for a few minutes. Strain the smoked haddock liquid into the pan, and keep cooking on a medium heat until the potatoes are tender and fully cooked. Finally, add the baby leeks and simmer for another 3 minutes until they are soft.

Season the cod and place it on a baking tray lined with greaseproof paper. Bake for 10 minutes.

When the cod is cooked, warm up the smoked haddock sauce. Add the spinach, chives and reserved smoked haddock flakes to the sauce and stir it through over the heat just enough that the spinach wilts, then pour plenty of sauce into each bowl and top with a piece of the fish.

Sea trout with razor clams and cockles

The key to cooking shellfish is a very hot pot! The cockles and clams add a lightness to this dish which otherwise is quite rich.

Clean the razor clams by standing them up in the sink so the bulbous end is pointing straight up. Leave the cold tap running: they'll suck up the water and 'spoot' it out, cleaning themselves while they're at it.

SERVES 4

4 sea trout fillets, weighing about 200g each
50g fine salt
800g potatoes
150g butter
100g double cream
400g Brussels sprouts, trimmed
½ tsp wakame powder
salt

SAUCE

1kg cockles
400g razor clams, cleaned
150ml white wine
2 shallots, thinly sliced
sunflower oil
100g fridge cold butter, cubed
salt

Check the sea trout fillets for any little bones. Mix the salt with a litre of water and put into a container, then submerge the fish in the brine for 30 minutes.

Transfer them on to a wire rack, skin side up, and place in the fridge for a couple of hours to dry out.

Preheat your oven to 180°c fan.

Pierce the potatoes all over and place on a tray in the oven for about 1 hour until cooked through. Cut them in half, scoop out the potato and push it through a potato ricer or mouli into a bowl. Warm 100g of the butter with the cream until the butter has melted, then gently fold the butter and cream into the potato with a wooden spoon or a spatula. Set aside until later.

Drop the oven temperature down to 170°c fan.

Halve the sprouts, then slice them thinly. Over a medium heat, melt the remaining 50g butter in a pot, then add the sprouts with the wakame powder and a good pinch of salt. Sweat down slowly until they are soft and cooked.

Put a deep pot with a lid over a high heat and let it get hot. Put in the cockles, razors and wine along with 200ml water and clamp on the lid. After 1 minute, check to see if the shellfish have opened. Carefully remove any that are open, and cook the rest for 1 more minute. Discard anything that stubbornly stays closed. Set the cooked shellfish aside to cool and pass the cooking liquor through a fine sieve.

Recipe contines overleaf

Over a medium heat, gently sweat the shallots down in a little oil and a pinch of salt until they are soft and transparent. Add the reserved shellfish cooking liquor, bring to the boil and reduce until the pan is almost dry, then whisk in the butter a few pieces at a time to get a glossy sauce. Pass through a sieve and taste to check the seasoning.

Pick the shellfish from the shells. Pull off the muscley pad from all the cockles and discard. Slice off the very top and bottom of the razor clams, then cut out the bulbous central section and discard. Slice the remaining razor meat on the diagonal into 1cm pieces. Add all the shellfish to the sauce.

Put a little oil in a frying pan – preferably one that can go in the oven – over a medium heat, then place in the sea trout fillets skin-side down. If the fish doesn't stay flat, carefully press it down with a fish slice, or take the pan off the heat for a few seconds and it will relax. Cook for a few minutes until the skin is nice and crispy, then flip the fish over and put it in the oven for 5 minutes (transferring it to a baking tray if you need to).

Warm up the potatoes, sprouts and shellfish sauce if they need a little reheating. Place a fat dollop of potato purée on a deep plate, then a layer of the sprouts, then the trout. Spoon the sauce and the shellfish all around and serve.

Halibut with artichokes and red wine sauce

Red wine sauce is an obvious choice to go with all different kinds of meat, but it is also wonderful with fish. Paired with creamy artichoke purée, it's a match made in heaven – rich, indulgent, naughty.

Salting the fish has many purposes: it allows the fish to be seasoned throughout rather than just on the surface, and it also helps lock in the moisture and proteins, which in turn means you'll have a juicy, tender piece of fish!

SERVES 4

4 halibut fillets, weighing about 200g each
50g fine salt
600g Jerusalem artichokes
juice of 1 lemon
2 tsp sunflower oil
500ml white chicken stock (page 278)
100ml milk
400ml red wine sauce
1 winter truffle

Cover both sides of the fish with the fine salt and leave in the fridge for 6 minutes. Wash the salt off in cold water, then lay the fillets on top of a wire rack over a tray and place back in the fridge to dry out a little until you're ready to cook them.

Peel the artichokes into a bowl of water with the lemon juice added – this helps prevent them from oxidising and turning brown. Chop them into 5mm slices. Add the oil to a pan over a medium heat, then add the artichokes and a pinch of salt and sauté for 5 minutes. Pour over the chicken stock and simmer until the artichokes are cooked and the stock has reduced to almost dry. Add in the milk, bring to a boil and reduce slightly. Blitz to a smooth purée, taste and adjust the seasoning if needed.

Preheat your oven to 170°c fan. Place the fish, skin side-up, on a piece of parchment on a baking tray and bake in the oven for up to 10 minutes depending how thick the fillets are (check it after 6 minutes). Carefully remove the skin. Warm the artichoke purée and red wine sauce if you need to, then serve each piece of fish with a dollop of purée and lashings of sauce. Finish with plenty of grated winter truffle.

Red wine sauce

This was one of the first sauces that I learned how to make, and I've lost count of how many times I've made it over the years. I love using Truefoods veal jus for my sauces – you can buy it online or in Waitrose.

MAKES ABOUT 400ML

4 tsp sunflower oil
4 banana shallots, thinly sliced
2 bay leaves
a small bunch of thyme
10 crushed black peppercorns
800 red wine (nothing fancy)
400ml veal jus

Heat the oil in a heavy-bottomed pot, then add the sliced shallots and sweat down with the bay leaves, thyme and crushed black peppercorns until soft.

Add in a third of the red wine, bring to the boil and reduce so the pan is almost dry. Add another third of the wine and again, reduce to almost dry. Pour in the remaining wine and reduce by half, then finally add the veal jus and gently reduce by half.

Pass through a fine sieve and serve.

Pappardelle with lamb shoulder ragout

You do really need a good-quality lamb stock rather than stock cubes here as it gets reduced down in the sauce. You can buy lamb bone broth online, or you could use 1.5 litres of Truefoods lamb gravy mixed with 1 litre of water.

SERVES 4

1 small lamb shoulder, weighing about 800g
1 tbsp fennel seeds
4 bay leaves
1 tbsp sea salt
1 fennel bulb, roughly chopped
1 onion, roughly chopped
2.5l lamb stock (page 278)
1 recipe pasta dough (page 281), rested
a little semolina flour
1 recipe pangrattato (see below)

Preheat your oven to 170°c fan.

Place the lamb shoulder in a deep roasting tin and scatter over the fennel seeds, bay leaves and salt. Add the chopped fennel and onion, then pour over the lamb stock and cover the tray with tin foil. Bake for 4 hours until the lamb is tender and falling off the bone.

Carefully remove the meat from the stock and let it cool enough to handle. Pick the meat off the bone and break it into smaller pieces with your fingers, discarding any sinew. Pass the stock through a fine sieve into a pot, and reduce until it has thickened to a good sauce consistency and tastes punchy but not too intense. Add the lamb and stir it through.

Now for the pappardelle. Cut the pasta dough into two pieces and leave one wrapped up in cling film. Flatten the other one to about 2cm thick with a rolling pin, then start feeding it through your pasta machine on the widest setting. Fold in either end of the pasta sheet so you have a triple layer, then feed it through the machine again. Now, change the pasta machine to the next setting and roll the pasta through twice, without folding it. Roll it twice through each remaining setting until it has gone through the second smallest, and you'll end up with a long, thin sheet of pasta. Square off each end of the pasta sheet and cut it into 20cm lengths then, with a pasta cutter, cut each length into pappardelle 5cm wide. Dust the pappardelle with a little semolina flour to prevent them sticking together. Repeat the whole process with the other half of the pasta dough.

Cook the pasta in a pot of boiling, salted water for 2 to 3 minutes. Drain and mix with the lamb ragout, then divide between your bowls and sprinkle with plenty of pangrattato.

Pangrattato

Pangrattato is a great way to put texture into food – I always add yeast flakes to bring an amazing umami taste.

MAKES ABOUT 65G

6 tbsp panko breadcrumbs
2 tbsp yeast flakes
½ tsp garlic powder
60ml sunflower oil

Mix together the panko, yeast flakes and garlic powder. Heat the sunflower oil in a frying pan, then add the panko mix and cook until golden brown and crispy, keeping the pan moving so it cooks evenly. Transfer to a sieve if there's a lot of excess oil; if not just drain on a couple of changes of kitchen towel.

Beef short rib and barbecue sauce

A warm hug: that's the best way I can think of to describe this dish. Tender meaty beef, punchy barbecue sauce and buttery mashed potato – everything I want to eat in winter, all on one plate. It's the dream.

SERVES 4

SHORT RIB

1.5kg short rib
1 garlic bulb, cut in half across
15g thyme
2 bay leaves
2l beef stock
sea salt
sunflower oil

MASHED POTATO

800g potatoes
200g butter
200ml double cream
1 tsp fine salt

BARBECUE SAUCE

500ml red wine vinegar
80g black garlic purée
80g tomato ketchup
70g light soft brown sugar
70ml maple syrup
1 tsp smoked paprika
1 tsp garlic powder
1 tsp onion powder
1 tsp mustard powder
1 tsp cracked black pepper
1 tsp sea salt

Preheat your oven to 165°c fan.

Season the short rib and place in a deep roasting tin with the garlic, thyme and bay leaves. Pour over the beef stock and cover the tin with tin foil, then put in the oven and cook for 5 hours until the beef is tender.

Pierce the potatoes all over with a fork and place on a baking tray. Bake at 165°c fan for 1 ½ hours, until they are cooked through. While they're still warm, cut them in half and scoop the soft flesh out, then pass it through a mouli or potato ricer into a bowl. Melt the butter with the cream and salt in a pot, then gradually mix it into the warm potato with a wooden spoon or spatula to get a soft, buttery mash. Set aside until you're ready to eat.

To make the barbecue sauce, put the red wine vinegar in a pot with 125ml water and the other ingredients. Bring to a boil, and reduce until it thickens to a glossy sauce.

When the beef has finished cooking, remove it from the tin and set aside to cool. Carefully pull the rib bones out and cut it into four even pieces. Pan fry in a little oil for 2 minutes on each side, until it's a little crispy all over. Pour over the barbecue sauce and get everything heated through.

Warm up the mash and put a good dollop in the bottom of each bowl, followed by a piece of beef and plenty of sauce.

Sweet eggy bread and poached pears

There's something really nice about getting stuck in to sophisticated kids' food on a cold winter's morning.

SERVES 4

POACHED PEARS
1l pear juice (or use apple if you can't find pear)
2 star anise
1 cinnamon stick
6 pears, peeled, cored and quartered

EGGY BREAD
4 eggs
100ml whole milk
30g sugar
½ tsp vanilla extract
½ tsp cinnamon
4 slices of sourdough bread
1 tbsp butter

TO SERVE
200g natural yoghurt
ground cinnamon

In a large pot, warm the juice, star anise and cinnamon stick over a medium heat.

Submerge the prepared pears in the pear juice and bring up to a simmer, then cook gently for 5 minutes. Check a piece to see if it's done – you want it to be just tender – and if necessary simmer for a little longer, keeping an eye out as they can easily overcook.

Remove the pears from the juice with a slotted spoon and, once they've cooled a bit, cut them in half lengthways. Reduce the juice down until it is syrupy, then discard the star anise and cinnamon.

In a flattish bowl, whisk the eggs, milk, sugar, vanilla and ground cinnamon together. One by one, dunk the slices of bread in the mix for 2 minutes, turning a couple of times so they are soaked through. Melt the butter in a frying pan and fry the eggy bread over a medium-high heat until golden brown all over, about 2 minutes on each side.

Pop the pears back in the reduced syrup and warm them through. Arrange them on top of the eggy bread with a good dollop of yoghurt and plenty of the syrup, then dust over some cinnamon.

Chocolate bundt cake with malt chocolate sauce

A lot of our holidays growing up were spent on the west coast of Scotland sailing. There was a hotel on Loch Melfort that we would often sail past, and my sister and I would plead with our dad to anchor the boat and go ashore. They served a chocolate fudge cake with hot, fudgy sauce and squirty cream from a can, and with my young, inexperienced palette it was outstanding! This is a nod to it.

I start the roasted vanilla Chantilly (page 251) first as you need to infuse the vanilla for 30 minutes, then it must be fridge cold before you whip it up.

SERVES 8 TO 10

CHOCOLATE BUNDT CAKE

50g cocoa powder plus 30g to dust the tin
150g 70% dark chocolate, roughly chopped
50g milk chocolate, roughly chopped
150g butter
2 vanilla pods
3 eggs
175ml sour cream
100ml sunflower oil
40ml strong coffee
150g caster sugar
150g light soft brown sugar
250g self-raising flour
1½ tsp bicarbonate of soda
½ tsp fine salt

MALT CHOCOLATE SAUCE

4 egg yolks
2 tbsp caster sugar
1 tbsp cornflour
600ml milk
300g Ovaltine powder
150g 70% dark chocolate, chopped
50g milk chocolate, chopped

bundt cake tin

Preheat your oven to 160°c fan.

Thoroughly grease your bundt tin, then heavily dust it with cocoa powder. This can be quite messy, and I've found the easiest way to do it is to hold the bundt tin over a large bowl. Put 30g cocoa powder in a sieve and shake it over the tin, then tap any excess out into the bowl. You'll need to do this a few times to get full, even coverage. Add any leftover cocoa to your cake batter.

Place the dark and milk chocolate into a pot with the butter and 100ml hot water. Put over a medium-low heat, letting the butter and chocolate melt, then whisk until shiny and combined.

Cut the vanilla pods in half lengthways and scrape the seeds out. In a bowl, whisk the eggs, sour cream, oil and coffee together until combined, then add the vanilla seeds. Add in the caster and light brown sugar and whisk until smooth, and then whisk in the melted chocolate and butter.

Sieve the remaining 50g of cocoa powder, flour, bicarb and salt into a big bowl. Scrape in the chocolate mix and whisk until you have a smooth batter. Pour the batter into your bundt tin and bake for 40 to 45 minutes, until a wooden skewer inserted into the deepest part comes out clean. Leave the cake to sit for 10 minutes in the tin, then carefully tip it out on to a wire rack and let it cool completely.

While the cake is cooling, make your malt chocolate sauce. In a bowl, whisk the egg yolks with the sugar and cornflour. Warm the milk and Ovaltine in a pot until the mixture is steaming and the Ovaltine has fully dissolved. Pour the hot liquid over the egg mix in a thin stream, whisking continuously. Pour it back into the pot and cook over a low heat, whisking all the time, until the custard has thickened. Put the chopped dark and milk chocolate into a bowl and then pour in the hot custard. Stir until the chocolate has fully melted and you have a thick, glossy sauce.

When the cake has cooled, put it on to a serving plate and pour some of the malt chocolate sauce over the top so it drips down the sides. Leave it to set for 10 minutes.

Serve in slices with a jug of warm malt chocolate sauce and a bowl of roasted vanilla Chantilly on the side.

Roasted vanilla Chantilly

MAKES ABOUT 750ML

6 vanilla pods
750ml double cream
3 tbsp icing sugar
1 tsp sea salt

Preheat your oven to 180°c fan.

Place the vanilla pods on a tray and roast for about 10 minutes, until they are crunchy. Cut them in half lengthways and scrape the seeds out. Put both the seeds and the scraped pods in a pot with the cream and add the sugar and salt. Warm until the cream is steaming but not boiling. Take off the heat and leave to infuse for 30 minutes, then strain the vanilla-scented cream into a bowl. Set aside to cool, then transfer to a tub and pop in the fridge to chill. When the cream is completely cold, strain it to remove the vanilla pods and then whip to soft peaks.

Vanilla panna cotta with rhubarb and hibiscus

Rhubarb and hibiscus is a flavour combination that appears on my restaurant menu every rhubarb season. You really need forced rhubarb here as it barely gets cooked – it's a pop of colour in the depths of winter.

SERVES 4

PANNA COTTA
2½ platinum gelatin leaves
300g double cream
100g whole milk
60g sugar
2 vanilla pods

RHUBARB AND HIBISCUS CONSOMMÉ
500g rhubarb
100g sugar
15g dried hibiscus

four individual serving glasses about 8cm in diameter

The panna cotta needs at least 4 hours to set so make it first.

Bloom the gelatine in a bowl of cold water for about 5 minutes. Put the cream, milk and sugar together and warm over a low heat – it needs to be warm enough to melt the gelatine but not hot. Squeeze any excess water from the gelatine and stir it into the warm cream until it has dissolved.

Halve the vanilla pods and scrape out the seeds with a sharp knife (keeping the pods for roasted vanilla cream on page 81 or to flavour sugar). Add the seeds to the mixture and put it into the fridge, getting it out to stir occasionally – you want it to be totally chilled (but not set) before you transfer it to your moulds as this will stop the vanilla from sinking to the bottom. Pour the mix into your serving glasses and pop in the fridge for about 4 hours to set.

Meanwhile, roughly chop 375g of the rhubarb and mix with the sugar in a heatproof bowl. Tie the hibiscus in a bit of muslin, add it to the bowl and cover with cling film. Set the bowl over a bain-marie and simmer for 2 hours, by which time the rhubarb will be sitting in a pure pink consommé. Squeeze out the hibiscus to get every bit of flavour and colour from it, then strain everything through a muslin into a bowl. Cut the remaining rhubarb into 5mm dice and add to the warm consommé, then put it into the fridge to chill for a couple of hours.

When you're ready to eat, spoon the rhubarb over the panna cotta and serve.

Coffee and chocolate mousse

Inspired by an espresso martini, but better!

SERVES 4

COFFEE AND CHOCOLATE MOUSSE
130g dark chocolate, roughly chopped
40g milk chocolate, roughly chopped
250ml whipping cream
3 tsp instant coffee granules
7 medium egg yolks
1 medium egg
90g sugar

RUM CARAMEL SAUCE
100g dark soft brown sugar
30g butter
1 tbsp water
95ml double cream
2 tbsp rum

TO SERVE
4 tbsp orange curd
50g hazelnuts, toasted and cut in half

Melt the dark and milk chocolate in a bain-marie. In a small pot, warm 50ml of the cream and add the coffee granules, stirring until they have dissolved, then set aside.

In a heatproof bowl, whisk together the egg yolks, whole egg, sugar and 60ml water. Put over a pot of simmering water and cook, whisking continuously, until the sabayon reaches 70°C.

Take off the heat and fold both the chocolate and coffee cream into the sabayon. Whip the remaining cream to soft peaks and add a large spoonful to the sabayon mix to loosen it. Then fold in the rest of the cream with a spatula, taking your time so it is thoroughly combined. Transfer to a container and put in the fridge to set.

While the mousse sets, make your rum caramel sauce. Place the brown sugar and butter in a pot with the tablespoon of water and let them slowly melt together over a medium heat. Bring to a boil, then pour in the cream and bring back to the boil. Take the sauce off the heat and whisk in the rum. Leave to cool, then chill in the fridge.

To serve, use a warm spoon to scoop the mousse on to your plates. Place a generous spoonful on each one, then wet the back of a spoon with warm water and make an indentation into the mousse. Spoon some orange curd into the hollow, drizzle the rum caramel around the mousse and finish with a sprinkling of hazelnuts.

Orange curd

MAKES ABOUT 300ML

2 oranges
100g butter, cubed
90g sugar
4 egg yolks, beaten
a pinch of citric acid

Juice and zest the oranges and measure out 75ml of the juice. Place the butter, sugar, beaten eggs and citric acid in a pot with the orange juice and zest. Cook over a low heat, whisking all the time, until the curd reaches 82°C and is nice and thick and coats the back of your spoon.

Remove from the heat and transfer to a bowl or jar. Press a piece of cling film on to the surface of the curd to stop it getting a skin and set aside to cool. Once it's at room temperature, put it in the fridge to set.

Winter dinner party menu

All three courses for this dinner party were inspired by dishes I created on BBC Two's Great British Menu, such a fun and crazy time. From colour wheels and Thermoses, to Bovril, beef pies and a Matilda cake – it was an experience like no other.

Cured halibut in a warm smokie sauce

A big satisfying pie with chips and salad

Multi-layered chocolate and sea buckthorn cheesecakes to finish.

Whisky and pear old fashioned

I come from a family of whisky drinkers so it seemed only fitting to include a whisky cocktail. This has the warmth you want, but there is a refreshing element to it from the Earl Grey and pear that I really like.

SERVES 6

210ml blended Scotch whisky
210ml pear cordial
150ml Earl Grey tea
1 lemon

six old-fashioned glasses

Pour the whisky, pear cordial and Earl Grey tea into a jug or bottle and place in the fridge to chill.

Fill your glasses with ice and pour over the cocktail mix. Using a peeler, cut long strips of lemon peel and twist them to release the natural oils over the top of the cocktails.

Pear cordial

The pear cordial will make more than you need but keeps well stored in the fridge and is great for soft drinks too, topped up with lemonade or soda.

MAKES ABOUT 600ML

400g pears
200g sugar
⅓ tsp citric acid

Roughly chop the pears, just discarding the stalks. Put into a pan with the sugar and 500ml water and simmer for 15 minutes over a medium heat. Pass through a fine sieve into a bowl and leave to cool.

In a cup or small bowl, mix the citric acid with 25ml water. Add this to the pear cordial, then pour it into a sterilised bottle or Kilner jar and store in the fridge.

Cured halibut with Arbroath smokie sauce

This is a simple dish to make and serve but it does take a bit of time – the halibut needs 4 to 6 hours to cure. However it works really well in a dinner party setup as everything can be made up to a day before, and everything apart from the sauce is served cold. The contrast of warm sauce and cool fish is lovely.

The chive oil makes more than you need but keeps for up to 4 weeks in the fridge.

SERVES 6

CURED HALIBUT
500g skinless halibut fillet
100g sugar
100g fine salt

ARBROATH SMOKIE SAUCE
200g baking potatoes
a pair of Arbroath smokies
175ml double cream
275ml whole milk

CHIVE OIL
100g chives
50g spinach
200ml sunflower oil

PICKLES
¼ cucumber
1 fennel bulb
1 baby leek
1 recipe pickle liquor (page 280)

1 punnet salty fingers or samphire
a few sprigs of red amaranth or other micro herbs

Remove any skin or bones from the halibut. Mix the sugar and salt together, then generously coat each side of the halibut with the cure and place in the fridge to cure. Curing time depends on the thickness of your halibut fillet: if it is about 2cm then leave it for 4 hours, and if it's more like 4cm then leave for 6 hours.

Once it's cured, wash the cure mix off with cold water and place the fish on a wire rack in the fridge for a couple of hours so it can dry out a little.

The Arbroath smokie sauce is thickened with mashed potato, and the best way to make mash is to bake the potatoes – it does take longer than boiling them but the result is much better. So, preheat your oven to 180°C fan, then prick the potatoes all over with a fork and bake them for an hour until soft all the way through. Keep them warm once they're cooked.

While the potatoes are baking, break the smokies into pieces with your hands and place in a pot – skin, bones, tail and all. Pour over the cream and milk and heat until almost simmering. Remove the pot from the heat and leave it to infuse for an hour. Strain through a sieve and discard the fish, then transfer the infused cream to a blender.

Scoop the cooked potato into the blender (discarding the skins) and blitz just until smooth and no more. Pass the sauce through a sieve and taste and adjust the seasoning if need be – smokies are salted so it shouldn't need it.

For the chive oil, blitz the chives, spinach and oil together until smooth. Pour into a pot and warm to 80°C, then pass through a muslin cloth into a bowl and chill over ice immediately.

Recipe contines on p264

Prepare your vegetables for the pickles. Peel the cucumber and cut it in half lengthways. Scrape out and discard the seeds, then cut the cucumber into 1cm pieces. Trim the fennel and discard the outer layer, then chop the rest into batons about 3cm long and 2mm thick. Trim the baby leek and discard the outer layer, then slice it into 5mm pieces. Bring the pickle liquor to a boil and pour it over the cut veg, then set aside to cool.

To serve, cut the halibut into six pieces weighing about 80g each. Transfer to your plates, then garnish the top with the pickles, salty fingers and red amaranth. Heat up the Arbroath smokie sauce. Pour about a teaspoon of chive oil into a small jug, then pour the smokie sauce in next and mix slightly with a spoon to get a marbled effect.

Pour sauce next to the fish and serve.

Braised beef and caramelised onion pie

The filling can be made the day before and used cold – in fact, the whole pie can be made the day before and kept in the fridge until you're ready to cook it.

Have fun with the pastry decorating! The key to golden pastry is a good egg wash – just egg yolk and a tiny splash of cream.

SERVES 6

PIE FILLING
1kg beef cheeks
2½ tbsp sunflower oil
2 carrots, peeled and roughly chopped
1 celery stick, roughly chopped
½ a garlic bulb
2 bay leaves
20g thyme
2l beef stock
200ml red wine
20 baby or silverskin onions, halved
300g celeriac, peeled and cut into 5mm dice
10 onions, thinly sliced
16 slices of pancetta (you can also use Parma ham or prosciutto)
salt

1 recipe rough puff pastry (page 282)
4 egg yolks, beaten
splash of double cream
sea salt

27cm diameter ceramic pie dish

Season the beef cheeks, then sear them in a hot pan with a tablespoon of the oil, getting a nice colour on each side. Transfer to a deep pot. Add the roughly chopped carrots and celery to the beef along with the unpeeled garlic, bay leaves and half the thyme sprigs. Pour over the beef stock and red wine and bring to a simmer, then cook gently until the meat is tender, about 4 to 5 hours. Keep checking after 4 hours – the cheeks are ready when the meat pulls away easily.

Meanwhile, make the rough puff pastry on page 282, then split it into three pieces, one weighing 500g and the other two split evenly. Shape into flattish discs and wrap them individually in cling film. Leave to rest for a couple of hours in the fridge.

When the cheeks are ready, remove them from the liquid with a slotted spoon and leave to cool enough to handle. With your hands, pick through the beef cheeks, removing any pieces of sinew and tearing the meat into 4cm pieces. Pass the cooking liquid through a sieve into a pot.

Add the halved baby onions to the beef cooking liquid and bring up to a simmer, then gently braise for 20 minutes until they are soft. Strain the baby onions and set them aside, then pass the cooking liquid through a sieve into a pot. Reduce the liquid to about 350ml, with a thicker sauce consistency. Check the seasoning.

In a wide pan, sauté the celeriac dice with a pinch of salt in ½ tablespoon of oil until cooked through.

Mix together the beef cheeks, braised baby onions, cooked celeriac and reduced sauce, then add the picked leaves of the remaining thyme. You can keep this in the fridge until you are ready to make the pie.

Recipe contines overleaf

For the caramelised onions, heat the remaining tablespoon of oil in a sauce pot, then add the thinly sliced onions and a couple of pinches of salt. Cook down over a medium heat for about an hour until the onions are golden brown and very soft. Keep stirring from time to time and lower the heat if it looks like anything is burning. Set aside.

Preheat your oven to 180°c fan.

Now build your pie. On a floured worktop, roll the 500g piece of pastry out so it is 5mm thick and large enough to line the pie dish and hang a little over the sides. Wrap it over your rolling pin to transfer it to your dish, and gently press it into place.

Line the pastry with the pancetta: imagine your dish is a clock, then put one piece of pancetta pointing to 12 o'clock with the thin end of the rasher in the middle of the dish and the other end overlapping the edge. Put another one pointing to 3 o'clock, then one to 6 and one to 9. Using the same idea, fill in the gaps so there is no pastry left visible. Add half of the beef cheek filling and smooth it flat with a spatula, then put in the caramelised onions and smooth them out. Cover the onions with the rest of the beef cheek filling, then fold the ends of the pancetta back over the top. Make an egg wash by beating together the egg yolks and cream, and brush plenty of it around the sides of the pastry.

Roll out one of the remaining pieces of pastry to get a circle about 30cm in diameter (a little bigger than your pie dish) and 2 to 3mm thick. Lay it on top of the pie and pinch the pastry edges together. Brush the top with another thick layer of egg wash. Finally, roll out the last bit of pastry and cut out whatever shapes you like to decorate the top of the pie. When the decorations are in place, give everything a final egg wash and sprinkle with some sea salt flakes.

Bake the pie for 45 minutes and allow it to sit for 10 minutes before serving.

Triple-cooked chips with Savora mustard mayo

Potatoes like a cool, dark environment but keep them out of the fridge – it messes with the sugar levels and can make them cook unevenly and burn. Maris Pipers make the best chips.

SERVES 6

1kg Maris Piper potatoes
800g beef drippings (or 800ml sunflower oil)
1 tsp salt

Peel and cut the potatoes into chips about 5cm long and 2cm wide. Blanch them in boiling, salted water for 5 minutes until they are soft on the outside but still firm inside. Drain off the water and then gently toss them around in the pot to fluff the outside of the chip, like you do when you make roast potatoes. Spread them on a baking tray to cool, then put them in the freezer for 2 hours.

If the chips have stuck together, separate them. Heat your beef fat or oil to 140°C. Carefully drop the chips in and cook for 9 minutes. Take the chips out of the oil and increase the temperature to 180°C. Cook them for 6 to 8 minutes more until golden brown and crispy.

Season the chips and layer them in a bowl with generous drizzles of Savora mustard mayonnaise.

Savora mustard mayonnaise

MAKES 170ML

2 egg yolks
1 tsp white wine vinegar
1 tsp salt
2 tbsp Savora mustard
100ml sunflower oil

In a small bowl, whisk the egg yolks, white wine vinegar, salt, and mustard together with a teaspoon of water. Slowly start drizzling in the oil, whisking continuously so the mayonnaise emulsifies. Taste and adjust the seasoning if required, and transfer to a piping bag.

Baby gem and watercress salad

I love pairing a salad with a pie – it gives the relief that is often needed, and the freshness of the buttermilk dressing amplifies it even more. It's also really simple!

SERVES 6

BUTTERMILK DRESSING
100ml buttermilk
100g crème fraîche
2 tsp white balsamic vinegar
2 tbsp olive oil
salt

2 baby gem lettuces
a handful of watercress
¼ tsp sea salt

In a small bowl, whisk together the buttermilk, crème fraîche, balsamic and olive oil and season with a pinch of salt. Taste and adjust the seasoning.

Separate the lettuce into leaves and toss with the watercress. Sprinkle over the sea salt, then dress with the buttermilk dressing.

Dark chocolate and sea buckthorn cheesecake

Desserts made in glasses are one of my favourite things for a dinner party as they're so easy to serve. Here it's also a great way to show off all the beautiful layers in the cheesecake. This dish does require time and patience, but you can do it all in advance and it's definitely worth it. Sea buckthorn has such an interesting flavour – strong, sour, a bit funky – and it's perfect matched with rich dark chocolate. You can find the bright orange berries on beaches on the east coast – watch out though as the stems are spiky!

SERVES 6

DARK CHOCOLATE AND
SEA BUCKTHORN CHEESECAKE
150g dark chocolate, roughly chopped
160g cream cheese
80ml double cream
60ml sea buckthorn juice

CHOCOLATE PRALINE FEUILLETINE
50g milk chocolate, roughly chopped
60g praline paste
30g feuilletine

SEA BUCKTHORN JELLY
2 platinum gelatine leaves
150g sea buckthorn juice

WHITE CHOCOLATE MOUSSE
2 egg yolks
70g caster sugar
1 platinum gelatine leaf
120g white chocolate, roughly chopped
70ml milk
225ml whipping cream

CHOCOLATE SOIL
20g ground almonds
20g sugar
2 tsp plain flour
1 tsp cocoa powder
15g butter, melted
15g feuilletine
sea salt

6 individual glasses, about 8cm in diameter and 10cm deep

You need to make this in stages over a few hours.

First of all, make the chocolate and sea buckthorn cheesecake that makes the bottom layer of the dessert. Melt the dark chocolate in a bain-marie. In a bowl, mix the cream cheese, double cream and sea buckthorn juice together until nice and smooth. Mix in the melted chocolate and transfer to a piping bag. Working quite quickly while the mix is still warm and soft, pipe about 70g straight into the base of each glass, then smooth down with the back of a spoon. If it's difficult to pipe, give it a massage in the bag to soften it up. Wipe any smears from the inside of the glass with a cloth and put into the fridge to set.

The next layer is the chocolate praline feuilletine. Melt the milk chocolate in a bain-marie, then add in the praline paste and mix together. Fold in the feuilletine flakes. Scrape the loose chocolatey mix on to a sheet of greaseproof paper and place another piece of greaseproof on top. Gently roll with a rolling pin to make a very thin layer of chocolate about 3mm thick. Put it in the fridge, still between the greaseproof paper sheets, for at least 30 minutes until it's hardened.

Recipe continues overleaf

Once the chocolate feuilletine layer is chilled, put it on to your worktop and peel off the top layer of paper. Working quickly, cut out discs the same diameter as your serving glass (use another of the glasses, if you have one) and neaten up the edges with a knife. Press on top of the chilled chocolate cheesecake layer. It doesn't matter too much if the chocolate feuilletine disc breaks – just fit the pieces together and press down so you have a flat, level layer with no gaps. Wipe the inside of the glasses again and put back into the fridge while you make the sea buckthorn jelly.

Bloom the gelatine in a bowl of cold water for about 5 minutes. In a pot, warm the sea buckthorn juice, then squeeze out any excess water from the gelatine and add it to the pot. Stir until it has fully dissolved, then put the jelly into the fridge for 10 minutes until it is cool but not set. Divide the jelly equally between the glasses, pouring a layer about 5mm thick on top of the chocolate feuilletine. Return to the fridge.

The next layer is the white chocolate mousse. In a bowl, whisk the yolks and sugar together. Bloom the gelatine in a bowl of cold water for about 5 minutes and put the roughly chopped white chocolate into another bowl.

In a pot, warm the milk until hot but not steaming. Pour it in a thin stream over the egg mix, stirring continuously. Return to the pan over a medium-low heat and cook, stirring all the time, until it reaches 82°C and is thick enough to coat the back of your spoon. Squeeze out any excess water from the gelatine and add to the pan, stirring until it is fully dissolved.

Pour the egg mix over the chocolate, making sure it's all submerged, and leave for 30 seconds. Stir until the chocolate is completely melted and everything is smooth and glossy. Whip the cream to soft peaks and gently whisk it into the warm chocolate mix until it's fully combined. It will be quite liquid, so pour a layer about 2½ cm thick into each glass, then wipe off any smears from the inside and return them to the fridge for at least 2 hours, until the mousse is firm to touch.

The final flourish is the chocolate soil. Preheat the oven to 160°C fan and line a baking tray with greaseproof paper.

In a bowl, mix the ground almonds, sugar, plain flour, cocoa powder and a pinch of sea salt together. Stir through the melted butter, then tip the mix on to the lined baking tray and spread into an even layer. Bake for 15 to 20 minutes, then leave to cool on the tray. Once cool, mix through the feuilletine flakes.

Just before you're ready to eat, take the glasses from the fridge and sprinkle a layer of chocolate soil over the top of each.

Core recipes

These are all staples in my kitchen and they appear frequently throughout the book.

Vinegar infusions

Simple, delicious, flavoursome – infusing vinegar is a great way to capture seasonal flavour. Here are a few combinations that I've used throughout the book, but the same method and ratios can be applied to all sorts of ingredients, so experiment.

Deciding which vinegar to infuse depends on what you would like to use it for – white wine vinegar and red wine vinegar are more savoury than the sweeter white balsamic, which is lovely in desserts. But don't get too hung up on it: all the vinegars will make a delicious end product. White wine vinegar, for example, is delicious with strawberries.

With any fruit (including stone fruits) use a ratio of 1:1 fruit to vinegar. If you are using herbs or leaves, you need a ratio of 1:2 herbs to vinegar. Just put the flavouring in a jar, pour over the vinegar and leave in a cool, dark place for a week.

ALL RECIPES MAKE 250ML

BLACKBERRY VINEGAR
250g blackberries
250ml white wine vinegar

STRAWBERRY VINEGAR
250g strawberries
250ml white balsamic vinegar

ELDERBERRY VINEGAR
250g elderberries
250ml red wine vinegar

LEMON VERBENA VINEGAR
125g lemon verbena
250ml white balsamic vinegar

DOUGLAS FIR VINEGAR
125g Douglas fir sprigs, needles stripped off and the twig broken into pieces
250ml white wine vinegar

Stocks

Of course stock can be shop bought if you're short on time, but if time allows it is extremely simple and satisfying to make.

Vegetable stock

MAKES ABOUT 3.5L

2 white onions, quartered
1 leek, quartered
3 celery sticks, halved
2 carrots, peeled, topped and tailed and halved
4 bay leaves
10 sprigs of thyme
10 black peppercorns

Place everything in a large pot with 4 litres of water and bring to a boil. Turn down the heat and simmer for 1 hour. Carefully strain the stock through a fine sieve into a bowl and leave to cool. Store in the fridge for up to 4 days.

White chicken stock

MAKES ABOUT 3.5L

1kg raw chicken carcasses or chicken wings
4 bay leaves
10 sprigs of thyme
10 black peppercorns

Place the chicken in a deep pot and cover with 4 litres of cold water. Bring to a boil over a medium heat, then skim off any impurities or scum and add in the bay, thyme and peppercorns. Simmer for 1 to 1½ hours until the carcasses break up easily.

Carefully strain the stock through a fine sieve into a bowl and leave to cool. Store in the fridge for up to 4 days.

Brown chicken stock

MAKES ABOUT 3.5L

1kg raw chicken carcasses or chicken wings
2 tbsp tomato purée
4 bay leaves
6 sprigs of thyme

Preheat your oven to 180°C fan.

Place the chicken carcasses on a roasting tray and roast for 15 to 20 minutes, until golden brown. Drain off any fat, then transfer to a deep pot and cover with 4 litres of cold water. Pour a little more water on to the warm roasting tray that had the carcasses in it and scrape up any residue, then add that into the pot.

Place the pot over a medium heat and bring to a boil. Skim off any scum or impurities, then add in the tomato purée, bay leaves and thyme. Simmer for 1 to 1½ hours, until the chicken carcasses break up easily.

Carefully strain the stock through a fine sieve into a bowl and leave to cool. Store in the fridge for up to 4 days.

Lamb stock

MAKES ABOUT 3.5L

500g lamb bones
500g lamb trim
sunflower oil
3 tbsp tomato purée
4 bay leaves
6 sprigs of thyme
1 tsp fennel seeds

Preheat your oven to 180°C fan.

Place the lamb bones on a tray and roast for 15 to 20 minutes, until golden brown.

Cut the lamb trim into 3cm pieces and sauté in a large pot over a medium heat with enough oil to over the base of the pot. Sauté until caramelised, then stir in the tomato purée and cook for a few minutes. Add the roasted lamb bones, cover with 4 litres of cold water and bring to a boil. Skim off any impurities and add in the bay leaves, thyme and fennel seeds. Turn the heat down and simmer for 2 hours.

Carefully strain the stock through a fine sieve into a bowl and leave to cool. Store in the fridge for up to 4 days. Scrape off any fat from the top of the stock before using it.

Beef stock

MAKES ABOUT 3.5L

500g beef bones
500g beef trim
sunflower oil
3 tbsp tomato purée
4 bay leaf
6 sprigs of thyme

Preheat your oven to 180°c fan.

Place the beef bones on a tray and roast for 15 to 20 minutes, until golden brown.

Cut the beef trim into 3cm pieces. Put a large pot over a medium heat, and add enough oil to over the base of the pot. Add the beef trim and sauté until caramelised, then stir in the tomato purée and cook for a few minutes. Add the roasted beef bones and cover with 4 litres of cold water. Bring to a boil, skim off any impurities and add in the bay leaf and thyme. Turn the heat down and simmer for 2 hours.

Carefully strain the stock through a fine sieve into a bowl and leave to cool. Store in the fridge for up to 4 days.

Fish stock

MAKES ABOUT 3.5L

2kg white fish bones
  (discard any heads, guts or roe)
200ml white wine
2 fennel bulbs, quartered
1 white onion, quartered
4 bay leaves
6 sprigs of thyme

Rinse the fish bones in cold water, drain and transfer to a large pot. Pour in the white wine and place over a medium heat, then reduce so the pan is almost dry. Pour in 4 litres of cold water and bring to a boil. Skim off any impurities and add the fennel, onion, bay leaves and thyme. Turn the heat down and simmer for 30 minutes, then take off the heat and leave to sit for 1 hour.

Carefully strain the stock through a fine sieve into a bowl and leave to cool. Store in the fridge for up to 4 days.

Pickle liquor

It's great to have a batch of this in the fridge, so you can knock up some pickles at a moment's notice! It will keep in a sealed jar for up to 4 weeks.

MAKES ABOUT 500ML

200ml rice vinegar
200ml cider vinegar
100g caster sugar
1 tsp fine salt
½ tsp dill seeds
½ tsp cumin seeds
½ tsp fennel seeds
2 bay leaves
10 sprigs thyme

Put the rice and cider vinegars in a pot with the sugar and salt and 100ml water. Bring to the boil, then add the dill, cumin, fennel, bay and thyme. Leave to infuse as it cools. Once at room temperature, pass the pickle liquor through a fine sieve into a jar.

Mayonnaise

This is a great base recipe that you can add all sorts of tasty twists to, from wild garlic mayo (page 75) to Savora mustard mayo (page 270). Hellmann's is good, but this is better.

MAKES 250ML

2 egg yolks
1 tsp white wine vinegar
1 tbsp Dijon mustard
200ml sunflower oil
salt

In a small bowl, whisk the egg yolks, white wine vinegar and mustard together with a pinch of salt and 1 tsp of water. Slowly drizzle in the oil, whisking continuously so the mayonnaise emulsifies. Taste and adjust the seasoning.

Fresh cheese

Incredibly simple and very versatile! Don't throw away the whey once you've strained the cheese: it freezes well and can be used in place of water in everything from caramel to sourdough to soups.

MAKES 135G

500ml milk
120ml buttermilk
50ml double cream
½ tsp fine salt
juice of ¼ lemon

Mix the milk, buttermilk, double cream and salt together in a pot and place over a medium heat. Heat the mix to 90°C and simmer for 20 minutes – it will curdle and separate into curds and whey. Line a sieve or colander with a muslin cloth and set it over a bowl, then pour through the hot buttermilk mix. Leave it to strain for at least 30 minutes to get a soft, crumbly cheese. For a firmer cheese cover the cheese with the edges of the muslin cloth and place something heavy on top. Leave to press overnight.

Transfer the cheese to a bowl and slowly mix the lemon juice in, then taste and add more if needed.

Pasta dough

My friend Kip and his wife, Giada, have a pasta shop in Edinburgh called Aemelia. He was kind enough to share his pasta recipe with me and it is now the only pasta recipe I use. The quality of the eggs is very important when you're making pasta: we always use Burford Browns in the restaurant. It also makes a real difference to use exact quantities of whole egg and yolk, so this is one occasion when you should get your digital scales out. Bear in mind that whole medium eggs weigh about 50g, and medium yolks weigh about 15g.

MAKES 520G

330g '00' pasta flour
160g whole egg
30g egg yolk

Put the flour in a bowl or a stand mixer with the dough hook attachment. Whisk the whole eggs and egg yolks together, then add them to the flour and mix until they're fully incorporated. Remove the dough from the bowl and knead it by hand on your work surface for about 5 minutes, until it's smooth and pliable. Shape into a ball and wrap in cling film, then place in the fridge to rest for a couple of hours before using.

Cream cheese pastry

This was one of my favourite recipes from my time at Twelve Triangles – salty, buttery, crumbly deliciousness! It makes twice as much as you need for the tarts on pages 159 and 160, but you can freeze the other half, well wrapped in cling film.

MAKES 500G

250g plain flour
½ tsp baking powder
½ tsp fine salt
½ tsp caster sugar
125g unsalted butter straight
    from the fridge, cubed
80g cream cheese
1 medium egg

Place the plain flour, baking powder, salt and sugar in a food processor and pulse a few times to mix everything evenly.

Add the butter and pulse until it's like breadcrumbs, then add the cream cheese and egg. Pulse very quickly until it just starts to come together, but be careful not to over mix. Turn it out on to your work bench and use your hands to mould it into two fat discs. Wrap them separately in cling film and rest in the fridge for at least 2 hours.

Rough puff pastry

MAKES ABOUT 800G

500g plain flour
250g cold salted butter, diced small
2 tbsp milk
3 medium egg yolks

In a stand mixer with the paddle attachment or by hand in a bowl, mix the flour and butter together until it forms a breadcrumb texture. Beat the milk and egg yolks with 80ml water and add it in, then mix until everything is just combined. Turn the dough out on to the worktop and finish it with your hands. Shape the dough into a rectangle, then cut it in half and wrap each piece in cling film. Put in the fridge to rest for at least an hour.

Sweet pastry

MAKES ABOUT 500G

120g butter, softened
60g icing sugar
1 egg
260g strong bread flour
salt

In a stand mixer, mix the butter and icing sugar together until just combined, then mix for 1 minute on medium speed. Add the egg and mix – don't worry if it looks curdled. Add the flour and a pinch of salt and mix until it is just combined. Empty the dough on to your worktop and shape into a flat disc with your hands, then wrap in cling film and rest in the fridge for at least 2 hours.

Index

A

almonds
   Mackerel with basil and smoked almond sauce 118
   Wild garlic soup with smoked haddock and almonds 42

apple
   Celeriac and apple soup with walnut crumpet 166
   Cured sea trout with apple 165
   Oysters with blackberry and apple 150
   Pork kofta with apple molasses 143

Apple and ginger loaf 186

Arbroath smokie
   Cured halibut with Arbroath smokie sauce 262

artichokes
   Halibut with artichokes and red wine sauce 242

Asparagus and roast chicken hollandaise 46
Asparagus bagna cauda 72
Autumn vegetable gratin 202

B

Baby gem and watercress salad 271
Banana chocolate chip cookie 63
Basil panisse 95

beans
   White beans and black pudding 231

beef
   Braised beef and caramelised onion pie 265
   Rib of beef with spring veg and anchovy butter 61

Beef short rib and barbecue sauce 246
Beef stock 279

beetroot
   Smoked duck and beetroot salad 218

berries
   Summer berries 127
   Summer pudding 133

black pudding
   Pork belly and black pudding purée 177
   White beans and black pudding 231

blackberry
   Oysters with blackberry and apple 150
   Pigeon, chicory and blackberry tarts 160

Blackberry cheesecake brownie 191
Blackberry compote 186
Blackberry vinegar 276

boudin
   Game boudin with polenta 174

Bowl of clams, ham and peas 116
Brining 24

broth
   Chicken and orzo broth 44
   Ham hock broth 224

Brown chicken stock 278
brownie, blackberry cheesecake 191

C

cake
   Apple and ginger loaf 186
   Chocolate bundt cake with malt chocolate sauce 250
   Gooseberry and Earl Grey Swiss roll 65

capers, crispy 179
Carrot and goat's cheese salad 162
Cauliflower with vadouvan butter 233

celeriac
   Venison tartare with smoked celeriac remoulade 199
   Whole roasted partridge with celeriac and greengages 185

Celeriac and apple soup 166

celery
   Oysters with tomato and celery 86

Chantilly, roasted vanilla 251

cheese
   Carrot and goat's cheese salad 162
   Fresh cheese 280
   Fresh cheese, tomato and courgette tarts 104
   Ox tongue and Cheddar cheese soldiers 213
   Pumpkin and fresh cheese tarts 159

cheesecake
   Blackberry cheesecake brownie 191
   Dark chocolate and sea buckthorn cheesecake 273

Cherry, pistachio and marzipan trifle 135

chicken
   Asparagus and roast chicken hollandaise 46
   Barbecued chicken thighs with date molasses 173
   Brown chicken stock 278
   White chicken stock 278

Chicken and orzo broth 44
Chicken liver parfait and peaches on toast 91
Chickpea pancakes with peas 34
Chicory salad with chestnuts and pumpkin seeds 203
chips, triple cooked 270

chocolate
   Banana chocolate chip cookie 63
   Coffee and chocolate mousse 257
   Dark chocolate and sea buckthorn cheesecake 273
   Hazelnut and chocolate Paris-Brest 204

Chocolate bundt cake with malt chocolate sauce 250

clams
   Bowl of clams, ham and peas 116
   Sea trout with razor clams and cockles 239

cod
   Baked cod with mussels, pancetta, cider and sage 200

Cod and cullen skink 236

coffee
   Spiced pumpkin and coffee panna cotta 192

Coffee and chocolate mousse 257
Cold smoking 22
compote, blackberry 186
Confit duck milk buns 154
cookie, banana chocolate chip 63

cordial
  Elderflower cordial 70
  Pear cordial 260
courgette
  Fresh cheese, tomato and courgette tarts 104
  Ricotta-stuffed courgette flowers with romesco 100
Crab thermidor muffin 226
Cream cheese pastry 281
cream, roasted vanilla 81
Crispy capers 179
crumpet, walnut 166
cucumber
  Oysters with elderflower and cucumber 28
Curing 23
Curried mussel soup 223
custard
  Raspberry custard tart 146

D

Damson gin 196
Damson negroni 196
Dark chocolate and sea buckthorn cheesecake 273
date
  Barbecued chicken thighs with date molasses 173
Devilled lamb kidneys and sweetbreads on toast 171
dinner party menus
  Spring dinner party menu 68
  Summer dinner party menu 138
  Autumn dinner party menu 194
  Winter dinner party menu 258
Douglas fir vinegar 276
duck
  Confit duck milk buns 154
  Mallard rillettes on duck fat toast 152
  Smoked duck and beetroot salad 218

E

eggs
  Ham hock rarebit with fried eggs 228
  poaching 23
  Sweet eggy bread and poached pears 248
elderflower
  Oysters with elderflower and cucumber 28
  Sake and elderflower fizz 70
  Strawberry and elderflower sundae 66
Elderflower cordial 70
Elderflower vinegar 276

F

fennel
  Whole roasted plaice with seaweed butter, fennel and orange 182
feta
  Whipped feta on toast with pickles 30
Filleting a mackerel 16
Fish finger sandwich 168
Fish stock 279
Flatbreads 73
Focaccia 92
frangipane
  Greengage frangipane tart 188
Fresh cheese 280
Fresh cheese, tomato and courgette tarts 104

G

galette, trout and spring vegetable 49
game birds
  prepping 18
  tying 20
Game boudin with polenta 174
gazpacho
  Herb gazpacho 41
  Sunflower seed gazpacho and grilled peaches 99
gnudi, watercress 113
goat's cheese
  Carrot and goat's cheese salad 162
Goat's cheese agnolotti with wild garlic sauce 54
Gooseberry and Earl Grey Swiss roll 65
gratin, autumn vegetable 202
green goddess
  Hake with green goddess 121
greengage
  Greengage frangipane tart 188
  Whole roasted partridge with celeriac and greengages 185
Grouse and tattie scones 110
guinea fowl
  Roast guinea fowl with peas and bacon 57

H

Haggis sausage roll 214
Hake with green goddess 121
halibut
  Cured halibut with Arbroath smokie sauce 262
  Halibut with artichokes and red wine sauce 242
ham hock
  Bowl of clams, ham and peas 116
  Ham hock broth 224
  Ham hock rarebit with fried eggs 228
Hazelnut and chocolate Paris-Brest 204
Herb gazpacho 41
hollandaise
  Asparagus and roast chicken hollandaise 46
Hot smoking 22

J

jalapeño
  Oysters with jalapeño hot sauce 210
John Dory
  Baked John Dory with seaweed Jersey Royals 58

K

Kedgeree 52
ketchup
  Pickled walnut ketchup 37
  Plum ketchup 155
  Turnip ketchup 215
kofta
  Pork kofta with apple molasses 143

L

lamb
  Devilled lamb kidneys and sweetbreads on toast 171
  Pappardelle with lamb shoulder ragout 245
  Roasted lamb rack with labneh and sweetheart cabbage 123
  Slow roast lamb shoulder and lamb fat potatoes 77
Lamb stock 278
Lanark Blue and nectarine tarte tatin 124
langoustine
  Red mullet with langoustine sauce 234
  Langoustines with wild garlic mayonnaise 75

INDEX

Lemon thyme parfait with grilled peaches 130
Lemon verbena vinegar 276
lobster, cooking and breaking down 14
Lobster rolls 107

M
mackerel
    Filleting a mackerel 16
    Smoked mackerel pâté with pickles 33
    Mackerel with basil and smoked almond sauce 118
Mallard rillettes on duck fat toast 152
Mayonnaise 280
mousse
    Coffee and chocolate mousse 257
muffin, crab thermidor 226
mushrooms
    Tagliatelle with wild mushrooms and garlic sauce 179
mussels
    Baked cod with mussels, pancetta, cider and sage 200
    Curried mussel soup 223
mustard mayonnaise, Savora 270

N
nectarine
    Lanark Blue and nectarine tarte tatin 124
negroni, Damson 196

O
octopus
    Barbecued octopus and tomatoes 114
orange
    Radicchio and orange salad 221
    Rhubarb and orange pavlova 80
    Whole roasted plaice with seaweed butter, fennel and orange 182
Orange curd 257
orzo
    Chicken and orzo broth 44
Ox tongue and Cheddar cheese soldiers 213
oyster, shucking 10
Oysters with blackberry and apple 150
Oysters with elderflower and cucumber 28
Oysters with jalapeño hot sauce 210
Oysters with tomato and celery 86

P
pancakes
    Chickpea pancakes with peas 34
Pangrattato 245
panisse, basil 95
panna cotta
    Spiced pumpkin and coffee panna cotta 192
    Vanilla panna cotta with rhubarb and hibiscus 254
Pappardelle with lamb shoulder ragout 245
parfait
    Chicken liver parfait and peaches on toast 91
    Lemon thyme parfait with grilled peaches 130
partridge
    Whole roasted partridge with celeriac and greengages 185
pasta
    Goat's cheese agnolotti with wild garlic sauce 54
    Pappardelle with lamb shoulder ragout 245
    Tagliatelle with wild mushrooms and garlic sauce 179
Pasta dough 281
pastry
    Cream cheese pastry 281
    Rough puff pastry 282
    Sweet pastry 282
pavlova
    Rhubarb and orange pavlova 80
peach
    Chicken liver parfait and peaches on toast 91
    Lemon thyme parfait with grilled peaches 130
    Sunflower seed gazpacho and grilled peaches 99
pear
    Sweet eggy bread and poached pears 248
    Whisky and pear old fashioned 260
Pear cordial 260
pea
    Bowl of clams, ham and peas 116
    Chickpea pancakes with peas 34
    Roast guinea fowl with peas and bacon 57
Pickled walnut ketchup 37

pickles
    Smoked mackerel pâté with pickles 33
    Whipped feta on toast with pickles 30
Pickle liquor 280
pie
    Braised beef and caramelised onion pie 265
    Scotch pies 37
Pigeon, chicory and blackberry tarts 160
plaice
    Whole roasted plaice with seaweed butter, fennel and orange 182
Plum ketchup 155
Poaching an egg 23
polenta
    Game boudin with polenta 174
Pork belly and black pudding purée 177
Pork belly B.L.T. 108
Pork kofta with apple molasses 143
potatoes
    Grouse and tattie scones 110
    Slow roast lamb shoulder and lamb fat potatoes 77
    Triple-cooked chips with Savora mustard mayo 270
Prepping a game bird 18
pumpkin
    Spiced pumpkin and coffee panna cotta 192
Pumpkin and fresh cheese tarts 159

R
Radicchio and orange salad 221
Raspberry custard tart 146
razor clams
    Sea trout with razor clams and cockles 239
Red mullet with langoustine sauce 234
Red wine sauce 242
rhubarb
    Vanilla panna cotta with rhubarb and hibiscus 254
Rhubarb and orange pavlova 80
Rib of beef with spring veg and anchovy butter 61
rice pudding, chilled 128
Ricotta-stuffed courgette flowers with romesco 100

rillettes
    Mallard rillettes on duck fat toast 152
Romesco sauce 101
Rough puff pastry 282

S

Sake and elderflower fizz 70
salad
    Baby gem and watercress salad 271
    Carrot and goat's cheese salad 162
    Chicory salad with chestnuts and pumpkin seeds 203
    Radicchio and orange salad 221
    Smoked duck and beetroot salad 218
    Tomato and watermelon salad 96
Salsa verde 44
Salting and brining 24
sausage roll, haggis 214
scallop, shucking 12
Scallops and sweetheart cabbage 51
Scotch pies 37
sea buckthorn
    Dark chocolate and sea buckthorn cheesecake 273
sea trout
    Cured sea trout with apple 165
Sea trout with razor clams and cockles 239
seaweed
    Baked John Dory with seaweed Jersey Royals 58
    Whole roasted plaice with seaweed butter, fennel and orange 182
Smoked duck and beetroot salad 218
smoked haddock
    Cod and cullen skink 236
    Cured halibut with Arbroath smokie sauce 262
    Kedgeree 52
    Wild garlic soup with smoked haddock and almonds 42
Smoked mackerel pâté with pickles and treacle soda bread 33
Smoking 22
soup
    Celeriac and apple soup with walnut crumpet 166
    Chicken and orzo broth 44

Curried mussel soup 223
Ham hock broth 224
Herb gazpacho 41
spring vegetables
    Rib of beef with spring veg and anchovy butter 61
    Trout and spring vegetable galette 49
squid
    Whole baked turbot with braised squid ratatouille 144
Strawberry and elderflower sundae 66
Strawberry and ginger hi-ball 140
Strawberry syrup 140
Strawberry vinegar 276
Stocks 278
Summer berries 127
Summer pudding 133
Sunflower seed dip 72
Sunflower seed gazpacho and grilled peaches 99
Sweet eggy bread and poached pears 248
Sweet pastry 282
sweetheart cabbage
    Roasted lamb rack with labneh and sweetheart cabbage 123
    Scallops and sweetheart cabbage 51

T

Tagliatelle with wild mushrooms and garlic sauce 179
tarts
    Fresh cheese, tomato and courgette tarts 104
    Greengage frangipane tart 188
    Lanark Blue and nectarine tarte tatin 124
    Pigeon, chicory and blackberry tarts 160
    Pumpkin and fresh cheese tarts 159
    Raspberry custard tart 146
thermidor
    Crab thermidor muffin 226
Toasting nuts and seeds 23
tomato
    Barbecued octopus and tomatoes 114
    Fresh cheese, tomato and courgette tarts 104

Oysters with tomato and celery 86
Tomato and watermelon salad 96
Tomatoes and tapenade on toast 88
tongue
    Ox tongue and Cheddar cheese soldiers 213
Treacle soda bread 33
trifle, cherry, pistachio and marzipan 135
Trout and spring vegetable galette 49
turbot
    Whole baked turbot with braised squid ratatouille 144
Tying a game bird 20

V

vadouvan
    Cauliflower with vadouvan butter 233
vanilla
    Roasted vanilla Chantilly 251
    Roasted vanilla cream 81
Vanilla panna cotta with rhubarb and hibiscus 254
Vegetable stock 278
Venison tartare with smoked celeriac remoulade 199
Vinegar infusions 276

W

walnut
    Celeriac and apple soup with walnut crumpet 166
    Pickled walnut ketchup 37
watercress
    Baby gem and watercress salad 271
Watercress gnudi 113
watermelon
    Tomato and watermelon salad 96
Whipped feta on toast with pickles 30
Whisky and pear old fashioned 260
White beans and black pudding 231
White chicken stock 278
wild garlic
    Goat's cheese agnolotti with wild garlic sauce 54
    Langoustines with wild garlic mayonnaise 75
    Wild garlic soup with smoked haddock and almonds 42

Thank you

Writing this book was everything I expected and so, so much more, and I couldn't have done it without all the wonderful people around me, past and present.

The biggest heartfelt thanks to:

All the guests who have eaten at the restaurants over the years and helped give me the confidence to write this book.

Rebecca Dickson, for creating the most beautiful and elegant images. We were always on the same page when deciding which was the perfect final shot and I can't think of anyone I would have wanted to work with more.

Maeve Emmott, for being the best wingwoman and morale booster. Her sharp eye and quick wit were the exact tonic that was needed in the depths of the long shoots, finishing each shot with 'I think this is my favourite …'

My publishers Emily and Nasim, for embarking on this journey with me with so much patience, knowledge and dedication. Relentless recipe testing, endless email threads, they helped turn my 'cheffy' writing into a beautifully scripted book.

The restaurant teams: I couldn't have written this book without them around me. Hamish – for helping me get through all the shoots and cooking so much food, Dom for being a constant inspiration and rock, and Sofia for putting up with the endless recipe testing in The Little Chartroom prep kitchen.

Dominic Jack and Tom Kitchin, my mentors who gave me a chance all those years ago and never held me back. Their knowledge, passion and drive was infectious and shaped me into who I am today.

Team Goya. I hummed and hawed a lot before making the decision to write this book, but Sara Al-Ali gave me the push I needed to jump over that last hurdle and say yes. Iona Fraser brought the initial idea to life with the exact clarity and vision I needed, and the whole team were a constant reassuring presence during all those conversations about titles and front covers.

Helen Glassford, for letting us use her stunning paintings that capture the rustic landscape and coastline of Scotland so beautifully, and reflect with perfect synergy the changing seasons throughout the book.

Clare Skeats who opened my eyes to the intricate finer details involved in designing books – I now look at books in such a different way.

My sister Alex for always being a comforting voice of reason and positivity, and for guiding me through life with such grace, style and elegance. For being by my side after Cara was born. For being the best big sister.

Mum and Dad, for their constant unwavering belief and support. From my first experience in a professional kitchen at 16, to moving to Dubai at six week's notice, through nine years with the Kitchin group and then opening The Little Chartroom, Eleanore and Ardfern, you've both been there for it all through the literal blood, sweat and tears, offering words of wisdom and comfort, creating beautiful artwork for our walls and bailing me out by driving to suppliers to pick up produce – thank you. For all the memories growing up – Saturdays at the factory, baking days with Gran Hall, barbecues off the back of the boat and buzzing around in small dinghies – thank you for giving me a story to tell.

And finally thank you to my amazing husband Shaun, my partner in every aspect of life, my greatest critic, and my strongest support. Thank you for every day over the last 11 years – each year has been a bit bigger and crazier. Thank you for pushing when you knew I could reach higher, for always striving to be better, and for keeping me up when I've stumbled.

Roberta x